The Legend of the Goddess

INVOKING SRI SUKTAM

The Legend of the Goddess

INVOKING SRI SUKTAM

OM SWAMI

JAICO PUBLISHING HOUSE

Ahmedabad Bangalore Chennai
Delhi Hyderabad Kolkata Mumbai

Published by Jaico Publishing House
A-2 Jash Chambers, 7-A Sir Phirozshah Mehta Road
Fort, Mumbai - 400 001
jaicopub@jaicobooks.com
www.jaicobooks.com

THE POWER OF MANTRAS
Book 3
THE LEGEND OF THE GODDESS
ISBN 978-93-49358-40-9
(3 Volume Set)

First Jaico Impression: 2025

Cover art (commissioned): loïc bramoullé
Cover design: Sushree Svadha Om
Sri Suktam verses at chapter beginnings:
Lakshmi Tantra translation by Sanjukta Gupta

Page design and layout: Jojy Philip, Delhi

Printed by
Parksons Graphics Pvt. Ltd., Mumbai

Contents

नमो नित्यानवद्याय जगतः सर्वहेतवे ।
ज्ञानाय निस्तरंगाय लक्ष्मीनारायणात्मने ॥

namo nityānavadyāya jagataḥ sarvahetave ।
jñānāya nistaraṅgāya lakṣmī nārāyaṇātmane ॥

I offer my obeisance to the eternally pure and unagitated Divine Mother who is the soul of Narayana, the foundation of existence, and absolute knowledge

Why This Book

Emerging from the sacred verses of the Rig Veda, Sri Suktam is one of the most ancient and powerful hymns in the world. This beautiful sadhana (spiritual discipline) grants you a rare glimpse into the radiant reflection of the Goddess's grace and benevolence. The sixteen verses of Sri Suktam were brought to life by various sages over the course of thousands of years.

There is also a beautiful story behind every verse, some unheard, some untold, but all true. Besides, my personal experience of Sri Suktam sadhana has been nothing but extraordinary. The manner in which this sacred hymn transforms your life is quite a phenomenon.

In the pages that follow, I bring to you the rich background, practice, and meaning of this splendid Vedic hymn—Sri Suktam.

All said and done, however, it's not an enviable position to be in. In fact, I find myself stationed in a realm far from admiration, if anything, I am nestled in the dense forest of pity. *Kahan Raghupati ke charit apara, kahan mati mori nirat samsara.* On the one hand is the resplendent saga of the Lord, and on the other hand is my consciousness entrenched in the labyrinth of existence. Can anyone with a tiny pair of eyes ever behold the boundless splendor of an ocean's expanse? Or fathom the depths by floating on the surface? How can I possibly extol the virtues of the Goddess who actually emerged from the core of the ocean of supreme consciousness? To expound on the glories of the Divine Mother is way above my pay grade, and yet, here I am, audaciously poised to embark on an expedition precisely as ineffable as that.

It is quite possible that you may never undertake the sadhana of Sri Suktam, but I promise you that by the time you finish reading this book, you will be amazed at the depth of wisdom in the Vedas and how various adepts worked painstakingly to bring this powerful hymn to life.

While its most common use is simply as a devotional Vedic chant, in reality, Sri Suktam is capable of turning one's fortunes around. In fact, all other things being equal, if someone asked me to give them just one sadhana for their material progress, without a moment's hesitation I would hand them the Sri Suktam.

In the tradition of Sri Vidya, it's also used as a way to make 16 different offerings (*shodashopachara*) to the Divine Mother. Whether this divine hymn is used as a simple chant or to make 16 offerings, both are genuine options. But the real potent use of its verses is to align the Universal energy to further your pursuits in the material world. And when it comes to that, the

Sri Suktam sadhana has no parallel, nothing that comes even remotely close.

In Pancharatra texts—those texts that predominantly pray to the *sātvik*, tranquil, aspect of Vishnu or Mother Goddess—Sri Suktam is used to awaken the power and energies of Lord Narayana, who is, verily, Mother Goddess Herself. Each verse also contains mantras any seeker can chant individually, independent of Sri Suktam. At the end of this book, I have provided the translation of each verse along with the mantras found in the verse.

I have woven my sentences with meticulous intent, paying careful attention to not use two words when I can do away with one. So I assure you that wherever I have written something in detail, it is because it's relevant to the overall purpose of the book you are currently holding in your blessed hands. And that is: to help you live a life full of divine love and abundance.

Without further ado, let's go back to one of the most defining moments in time, the moment when Devi first emerged and the sublime hymn was revealed to the world.

हिरण्यवर्णां हरिणीं सुवर्णरजतस्रजाम्
चन्द्रां हिरण्मयीं लक्ष्मीं जातवेदो म आवह ॥१॥

hiraṇya-varṇāṃ hariṇīṃ suvarṇa-rajata-srajām ।
candrāṃ hiraṇ-mayīṃ lakṣmīṃ jātavedo ma āvaha ॥ 1 ॥

Immanent in all beings and I hum like the female bumble bee. As kundalini, I unfold myself with the brilliance of thousands of risen suns, fires and moons. On entering the last stage of (mantra) sound, I become the mother of all sounds, showering objects of enjoyment in the same way as a cow showers milk. Having praised me, addressing me as Hiranyavarna, the very wise Prajapati obtained my grace and became the narrator of the yoga religion.

Like a doe I flee farther and farther from the mind of the yogin. Yogins observing their vows bind me through their own devotion.

The Origin of Sri Suktam

Verse 1

Shiva wanted to maintain his distance from the monumental endeavor of the Devas and Asuras. He had no personal favorites nor was it possible to lure the Mahayogi. "I respect what you are trying to do," Shiva said to the assembled Devas. "But I doubt your intentions."

The Devas knew that there was no point in hiding anything from him. Unlike Vishnu, he did not lean towards the Devas. If anything, Shiva had openly supported and endorsed other species of Rakshasas and Gandharvas. Not to mention, his own tribe, the Rudras. Anyone and everyone who had ever been cast out by any other tribe found refuge in his. Shiva knew from the outset that the mighty Asuras would be outplayed by the Devas. And yet to show his support to both sides, he had agreed to camp close to the site till the churning was done. His only condition was that he would not participate in Samudra Manthan, or oversee it.

"Hey Pashupatinath, you alone can help us, O Mahadev!" Indra pleaded. "You are omniscient. We are doing this churning for the welfare of the world. But we cannot continue unless you take care of *halāhala*, the venom. Its fumes are rendering everyone unconscious. One spilled drop has turned several thousand miles of land barren."

Shiva knew they were telling the truth, but he asked Indra that if it was so important, why didn't Vishnu accompany him instead of sending him with the other Devas? Vishnu, on the other hand, knew that the first yogi would do anything if he asked for it personally, but that was precisely the point. Vishnu did not want to ask Shiva to do anything that he wouldn't do of his own volition. He trusted Shiva's penetrating insight, his yogic prowess, and his foresight. If Mahadev's turning down the request of the Devas meant that the Universe would come to an end, then so be it.

"O Bholenath," Indra said, "we did request Vishnu but as you know he does not disclose his mind or his reasoning. He simply instructed me to approach you."

And Indra fell at Mahayogi's feet. He knew that the only way to melt the nonpartisan Shiva was with pure devotion and in that moment Indra, the king of the Devas, felt nothing but extraordinary devotion. Mother Goddess, Uma, disapproved of Shiva taking care of the poison that had emerged from the churning of the ocean. She felt her Bholenath Shankara was being tricked.

Varānane, Shiva said to her in silence, *forget the* halāhala *from this churning, your Shiva can drink all the universes that have ever existed, with everything in it.* With that playful and serene yet sombre look, he induced in her a sense of ease. Besides, she well knew that Shiva was a force unto himself. She briefly rested her gaze on his matted locks that contained the mysteries of billions of cycles of creation and destruction. She knew that Shiva was not someone anyone could stop.

"You carry on," Shiva said to Indra. "I'll see you at the site."

Singing eulogies and glories of the Mahayogi, the Devas went back to the site of the churning. Samudra Manthan—the great churning of the ocean—is one of the most foundational episodes in the evolution of the Vedic era. To understand the subtler nuances and extraordinary chronology of human progress captured in Sri Suktam, we have to go back to Vedic history a little bit. Just a little bit.

From around 2 million years ago to as late as 110,000 years ago, there was a species called *Homo erectus*. These were ape-like creatures with features somewhat similar to modern human beings; they were known by the species name *erectus* because they could stand on two legs. From quadrupeds, they had become bipeds. This species is documented as Vānaras in our scriptures. Yes, the same ones who fought against Ravana.

Around the same time, there was another kind of human species, known as *Homo heidelbergensis*. The modern ring to this name is owed to a place called Heidelberg in Germany. Over a century ago, they discovered in this region fossils of people who existed on earth somewhere between 2 million to 600,000 years ago. *Homo heidelbergensis* formed the Gandharvas, Yakshas and Rakshasas. Asuras (loosely translated as "demons" in English) was another name for Rakshasas.

And then there were the Neanderthals. *Homo neanderthalensis* existed between 800,000 years to 40,000 years ago. They are what we classify as Devas in the Vedas.

The great churning of the ocean happened approximately half a million years ago. *Homo sapiens*—present day humans—

were a minority back then and we mostly lived in territories that were either unclaimed by anyone, or on land the Asuras and Devas had released for our use. So, the great churning had materialized after painstaking execution of diplomacy spanning several centuries. And it was guided by the most brilliant and versatile Vishnu. He was the common factor, trusted and loved by everyone.

As for the Asuras, they needed the brains and technology that the Devas possessed. With Vishnu's assurance, they reluctantly agreed to participate in an endeavor where different species had to come together to pull off the most daring feat of all time—Samudra Manthan. Vishnu knew that the Devas would need the might and brawn of the Asuras to *churn the ocean*, which required enormous physical resources and skill.

The site of the ocean churning was truly magnificent.

Shiva rode through the large congregation of Devas and Asuras. There were thousands upon thousands of them. They stood in awe and reverence, knowing it was none other than Maha Rudra, the greatest yogi, galloping on his bull, kicking up a storm. The adjacent land had somewhat singed, the plants had wilted, and the fruits had turned black. *Indra was not exaggerating, the venom is wildly poisonous. Why Vishnu plays all these games is beyond me.*

"Mahadev!" Vishnu embraced Shiva as soon as he dismounted Nandi.

Shiva peered deeply into Vishnu's twinkling eyes. There were abundant questions, bemusement and love in that gaze. Vishnu, as usual, just answered everything with that smile of his that could turn the deadliest venom into the sweetest nectar.

"I am doing this only for you, Padmanabha," Shiva said, wagging his finger. "What joy do you get from all these elaborate games?"

"It is your generosity you say that, Bholenath," Vishnu retorted and chuckled. "We know you are doing this for the welfare of the multiverse. You are doing this so creation can go on."

"I think someone is forgetting," Shiva countered, "that my job is to trigger destruction, not creation."

In the middle of such a dire situation, only these two could afford to be playful. Playfully was how they did everything, anyway. *Pralaya*, destruction, was Shiva's *leela*, play, and *stithi*, sustaining the creation, was Vishnu's.

Shiva went closer to the site. The great serpent, Vasuki, was wrapped around the tall Sumeru, the dasher, and the Asuras and the Devas were at each end with Asuras holding Vasuki's head and Devas, the tail. Each time they pulled and pushed, Vasuki would breathe a venomous puff which had made things rather difficult for the Asuras. They realized much later that the Devas had cleverly got them to join the churning in pulling Vasuki's head, at the receiving end of the toxic blast.

A *kūrma*, a giant tortoise, sat at the base of the mountain to give it stability. Samudra Manthan was the greatest and biggest project of hydro-engineering at the time. Everyone was exhausted already, and in their wildest dreams, they hadn't imagined that one of the first things to emerge from the churning would be venom so poisonous that even Vasuki could die from it. Dumping the venom irresponsibly was akin to leaving a vast amount radioactive waste in the middle of a city. But thankfully, Mahadev was now here.

Vishnu embraced Shiva once again. Suddenly his smile disappeared and his eyes welled up. Before long, a pair of tears trickled down Vishnu's ruddy cheeks. He knew what an extraordinary sacrifice the Mahayogi was about to make. And for what? Shiva certainly didn't want anything out of it all, nor did he have anything to gain from it. Shiva broke from Vishnu's embrace and gazed at him with admiration and love. If Vishnu was *giridhar,* bearer of the mountain (as Kūrma and later as Krishna), the other was *giripati,* lord of the mountains, of Kailasha. Both were playful, free, and yet bound by dharma. Neither had a personal motive and yet here they were.

Drinking the poison, Shiva would house it in his Vishuddhi chakra, the throat plexus. Should it go upwards and hit the brain, it would make him dizzy, which wasn't going to be good for anyone. If the venom went downwards to his stomach, it would eventually leave some residue in the form of a body fluid, which would be just as catastrophic for the world.

The Asuras and Devas thundered, "Har Har Mahadev! Har Har Mahadev!" Amid the deafening chants of 'Har Har Mahadev, Jai Mahakal, Har Har Mahadev, Jai Mahakal!' Shiva put the bowl of venom to his lips.

A hushed reverence descended as the Mahayogi continued to drink the *halāhala*. For a moment, it felt as if a billion galaxies held their breath as the Devas looked on in awe, witnessing the selflessness of a deity who bore the weight of the world.

Shiva's throat turned a deep blue by the time he had finished. And Vishnu named him 'Neelakantha', the one of blue throat.

No sooner did he finish, than Shiva quietly patted and mounted the teary-eyed Nandi. Through the rallying cries of his names, he left as quietly as he had come. Vishnu's heart was a bit heavy. The daft Asuras, believing it was no big deal for their omnipotent deity Shiva, went back to tending their other unconscious fellows who were now waking up as the effects of the venom wore off. The self-serving Devas rejoiced in the resolution of the monumental problem, and got on with the task at hand.

With the lethal poison out of their way, even Vasuki's breath was no more than a whiff of warm air now. The Devas happily agreed to change sides, giving the Asuras Vasuki's tail. The innocent Asuras mistook this as a great gesture of camaraderie and sacrifice by the Devas. The churning resumed, they once again got on with the gigantic task of pulling back and forth, back and forth, creating tremendous tumult in the cosmic waters.

The Asuras were certain that this joint endeavor would make them equal to the Devas, that they too would find an honorable and befitting mention in the Vedas. But their confidence was misplaced.

For a moment, think of the Vedas as the books of constitution. Not just political constitution, but something like our history books. That is, the Vedas have documented or compiled information about peoples, their ancestors, cultures, popular songs, wisdom and the rest. Almost like an anthology. Just as we have history books nowadays, we had the Vedas to document who and what were present in those times. The enormity of it all is simply mind-blowing.

As the churning progressed, first appeared the magnificent cow, Kamadhenu. Her luminous hide exuded an iridescent glow as if she held within her the very form of every material blessing anyone could ever need. Her horns were as if the perfect arches to the gates of heaven. Due to the heady fragrance she emitted, which was a welcome change from the noxious venom, she was given the name 'Surabhi'. Her benevolent gaze out of her innocent eyes immediately absorbed everyone's tiredness. Brahma accepted Surabhi and immediately passed it onto Brihaspati, the guru of the Devas. Eventually, at the emergence of *Homo sapiens*, Kamadhenu would end up with the great sage Vasishtha.

The churning resumed and next came the marvelous equine, Uchchaishravas. If Kamadhenu represented all feminine beauty, Uchchaishravas—the white stallion—appeared as if he contained all the masculine strength and poise in the Universe. He was so named because of his loud neighing and his beautiful long ears, both of which were called *uchchai-shravas*. White as freshly fallen snow shimmering under the full moon, Uchchaishravas was unlike any other horse anyone had ever seen. King Bali, the king of the Asuras, immediately expressed a desire to own the steed.

Indra wanted the stallion too, but Vishnu advised him to be quiet and let Bali have it. Later, when he would incarnate in his Vāmana *avatara* and Bali would lose everything, Uchchaishravas would end up with Vishnu, who would then pass it onto Indra. Vishnu had already foreseen this, and he knew that it was best for Indra to wait for now. Throughout Vedic history, in none of his incarnations or elsewhere, would he ever reveal anything ahead of its due time, or a smidgen more than what was necessary. Such were his ways and they suited him perfectly.

The Asuras and Devas reinitiated the swirling only to stop at the emergence of the majestic Airavata, the great white elephant with four tusks. Before anyone could express their desire to have the pachyderm extraordinaire, Indra put his foot down and claimed it for himself.

Next came more elephants, eight male and eight female, followed by precious gems out of which *kaustubha mani* and *padmaraga mani* were offered to Vishnu. Then emerged Parijata, a flower that would never wilt or lose fragrance, followed by a slew of Apsaras—celestial nymphs and damsels—that took their breath away.

A vision of ethereal allure, their diaphanous raiment traced every contour of their spellbinding forms—voluptuous, well-endowed, and well-proportioned—conducting a symphony of desires unknown to anyone present there. Anyone except Narayana, the very Vishnu who was beyond desire. Why, *he* was an embodiment of every desire ever possible in cosmic consciousness.

The Devas and Asuras stood with their mouths agape. The strapping, brawny and mighty Asuras were certain that the nymphs would choose them over the slender Devas. But the Apsaras chose the Devas for their charming, tender and regal looks. They related more closely with the Devas. This really upset the Asuras because for that brief period of time, they forgot all about the elixir, the chalice of nectar—*amrita*—

which was the chief object of the churning. All they wanted was to take those nymphs and go back to their kingdom. As far as they were concerned, this was the only nectar they ever needed. If not for the wise counsel of their guru, Shukracharya, they might have started a war right then and there.

"You silly bunch of bullhorns," Shukracharya whispered to them. "Don't you know that you cannot make a woman yours by force. You will have the bodies of the nymphs but they will hate you, and will flee the first chance they get. It's better to be chivalrous, generous and delightful than any other alternative. You may still have a chance with them in the future, then."

Most reluctantly, they agreed. Plus, they knew that the beautiful damsels would make their own wives back home insecure, which would turn every potential pleasure into absolute hell. *We might as well have drunk the poison. Besides, what are we gonna do with any nectar if we can't have these beautiful maidens. What could possibly be more worthwhile, beautiful or appealing than them?*

The Asuras lost all motivation to continue and the Devas couldn't wait to get back to Amaravati so they could indulge in untold pleasures—the latter completely forgetting that debauchery was the reason they lost their power in the first place. Shukracharya pulled up the Asuras and Brihaspati, the Devas, and the churning resumed. It felt like a draggy and slow affair now.

But nothing could have prepared them for the sight that came next. It was as if the whole Universe came to a complete standstill. An extraordinary figure emerged from the ocean, as if all the beauty in the entire creation had assumed one feminine form. It was as though the sun on the horizon ascended upon divine instruction and melted into gold as it poured at the site of the churning, raising a figure of unparalleled glamor and grandeur.

The light of all lights, she was none other than Sri, the goddess of fortune, of opulence. Called Ramā as she completely delighted everyone's heart, she was *bhagavat-para*, only to be had by the supreme lord. *Vidyut-saudamani*, she appeared suddenly like a bolt of electricity, vastly surpassing the magnitude of lightning ever witnessed before.

If the Apsaras had evoked every desire, the appearance of Mother Goddess totally overwhelmed them all. It was absurd for anyone, except Vishnu, to even imagine having her. "She is way above our pay grade," the Asuras murmured. "She is just not in our league," the Devas mumbled. But secretly, everyone thought that who knew they might just win the lottery. They would have gladly fought each other until the end of time, had the Goddess so indicated with an ever so slight arching of her eyebrows.

Draped in resplendent garments woven from silken and golden threads, studded with precious stones, the very air around her reeked of prosperity and opulence. As a divine aura enveloped her form, all who beheld her knew they were looking at a goddess, destined to bestow unimaginable riches, affluence, and abundance on anyone she found worthy.

She was *ranjayanti*, her countenance gleamed with the luminescence of a thousand constellations. She looked around as time stood still. Her divine form commanded such reverence and submission, that the Devas, Asuras and every creature present there wanted to serve her with everything they had.

Indra brought a throne for her, the Gandharvas began playing the most mellifluous of music, the Asuras offered their crowns at her feet, the sages started chanting, the Devas arranged for food, flowers, perfumes and more gemstones for her. Unanimously the sages called her Lakshmi, that is, she is everyone's *lakshya*, goal. But the goddess stood still, looking around. She was not after these offerings and riches. She was the goddess of wealth and fortune, after all. She was looking for something else, someone else. Someone who was beyond all these things. She needed someone to whom she could surrender, someone who could charm her with his sovereignty, genius, and wit. She did not want somebody who became subservient at the mere sight of her. But where was this faultless person?

She began moving about, in graceful doe-like steps. *Utpala-srajam-nadad-dvirephām*, holding a garland of lotuses with constantly circling bumblebees, she was *savrīda-hāsam*, smiling with shyness. *Sukapola-kundalam*, her dangling earrings would occasionally hit against her tender sanguine cheeks, adding to her natural beauty.

Moving through the Gandharvas, Asuras, Devas and sages—most of whom held their breath and pacified their thumping hearts with an internal dialog—the goddess stood still when she came near Vishnu. It was a no-brainer. She felt all those emotions for Him that others had been feeling for her until a few moments ago. Only, the intensity of her feelings was infinitely more than all of theirs put together.

She garlanded Vishnu with the lotus flowers that were still surrounded by humming bumblebees. She stood there reticently, with a demure smile. This was the only smile the Devas and Asuras saw that could be compared to that of Vishnu's.

Even the all-knowing Vishnu was radiating a warmth and joy the Devas had never seen before. The ever-working Narayana, it seemed, paused the wheel of time as he cast a brief gaze in the direction of Mother Goddess, Sri. Then, realizing that he was under the keen eye of the Devas and Asuras, he smiled one more time. But that one smile was enough for the Goddess to be put completely at ease, to be reassured that if there was anyone to whom she belonged, it was Narayana.

"Jai Jai Lakshmi Narayana!" Brahma shouted.

"Jai Jai Lakshmi Narayana!" everyone chanted in chorus.

The whole environment lit up with eclectic chants; the Devas blared the conches, the Asuras blew the trumpets, the Gandharvas played the mridangam, drums, and varied string instruments.

From that soft ground where Lord Vishnu and Lakshmi stood, two divine sages—Chiklīta and Kardama—emerged. They were immediately regarded as the sons of Lakshmi-Narayana. Pin-drop silence ensued once again at the appearance of these youthful sages.

हिरण्यवर्णां हरिणीं सुवर्णरजतस्रजाम् ।
चन्द्रां हिरण्मयीं लक्ष्मीं जातवेदो म आवह ॥

hiraṇyavarṇāṃ hariṇīṃ suvarṇarajatasrajām ।
candrāṃ hiraṇmayīṃ lakṣmīṃ jātavedo ma āvaha ॥

Invoke for me, O Agni, the Goddess Lakshmi who is radiant like gold, beautiful yellow in hue, adorned with garlands of silver and gold, magnanimous like the moon, and an embodiment of wealth and prosperity.

Chiklīta's voice, as if that of moving rainclouds, reverberated throughout the Universe as he called out to the goddess, his mother, with the aforesaid verse. This became the first of 16 verses of the sonic form of Mother Goddess. The entire hymn came to be known as Sri Suktam and each verse of this powerful ode is invoked by a different sage. Some sages have invoked more than one verse, and they are regarded as the seers of those verses. Every time the verse or the individual mantras are brought to life, the *rishi,* seer of the mantra is acknowledged and invoked too.

Na bhūto na bhavishyati, never before and not ever again, would this rare event occur. Chiklīta's chest heaved with a sense of accomplishment, pride and reverence, all at once, as he found himself occupying a very special place in Vedic history.

As Chiklīta chanted the first verse, the Devas, Asuras and sages stood with their heads bowed and hands folded. The sages saw in their mind's eye how the verse had seven hidden mantras, each one capable of transforming one's fortune. By the time the invocation of the first verse finished, it was evident to the seers gathered there, that this was not just a hymn but the script to rewrite anyone's destiny. They knew that it was an unrepeatable and unique moment in the history of the Universe.

Deep in their hearts, the entire assembly of august beings understood beyond any doubt that since it was not possible for the goddess of fortune to be with everyone physically, she could be invoked in her sonic form by anyone, anywhere, and be rewarded with wholesome wealth and prosperity. They knew that to make this world move—a world free from poverty—was only possible if wealth flowed freely.

But it was not all so easy. For, invoking each verse was like churning the ocean all over again. Figuratively speaking, of course. The great sage Chiklīta had brought the first verse to life, now someone else had to carry on the baton. But who? And when?

तां म आवह जातवेदो लक्ष्मीमनपगामिनीम् ।
यस्यां हिरण्यं विन्देयं गामश्वं पुरुषानहम् ॥२॥

tāṃ ma āvaha jātavedo lakṣmīmanapagāminīm ।
yasyāṃ hiraṇyaṃ vindeyaṃ gāmaśvaṃ puruṣānaham ॥ 2 ॥

Ever in motion, I destroy the afflictions of my devotees. Characterized by the vibrating happiness in the minds of the yogins, I rise and like the rising moon illuminate their fourth (i.e. turiya) state of consciousness. When the noble sage Vasiśtha was struck by the calamity hindering his yoga, reflecting on me, the pure one, the internal moon, he recovered his own yogic (capacity).

I, the witness abiding in all beings, notice what is good and what is evil. I am Hari's eternal majesty and I am the object of all cognitive knowledge.

The Temptress

Verse 2

"Resume the churning," Vishnu hollered.

Indra and Bali looked in the direction of their gurus, who wasted not a moment to nod in approval. The Devas and Asuras carried on with the task.

This surprised Lakshmi a little bit. She, the Mother Goddess, a consort of the supreme soul, had hoped that both Narayana and she would leave for Vaikuntha, immediately. The heart and soul of *samudratanaya,* the daughter of the ocean, was aflutter with dreams of serving Vishnu, of being with him in a timeless embrace. The last thing she had ever imagined was to be surrounded by vast numbers of men in the middle of what looked like a giant excavation site. But when did Vishnu ever leave anything unfinished.

Not oblivious to the gossamer web of thoughts of the goddess, an enigmatic smile made a fleeting appearance on Vishnu's lips as his gaze met hers. A silent acknowledgment passed between them, as if a promise of destiny about to unfurl. The goddess felt a wave of love swell in her heart. They walked to the encampment in graceful steps and took their seats.

Upekshitah Lakshmya—neglected by the Goddess, a bit demotivated and frustrated, also *nirudyoga*—feeling less industrious, the Asuras rejoined the effort of churning. Before long, another female form emerged from the ocean.

"We don't care who she is or what she wants," the Asuras said to their guru, Shukracharya. "We don't even care what she looks like. All we know is that she is coming with us."

This was Varuni, the seductress maiden, who represented slosh and inebriation. The Asuras were delighted to see her, and they were determined not to let the Devas or Vishnu have her. Varuni consented to be with the Asuras, and their king Bali, was only too pleased. About time they got someone beautiful too, they thought. The Asuras surrounded her.

"Pay attention, you goofballs," Shukracharya chastised them. "You are here for the elixir of immortality. Any moment now. Get back to the churning."

The Asuras believed they had been dealt a bad hand, as all the wonderful things from the Samudra Manthan were taken by the Devas. And yet, at the instruction of their guru and the order of their king, they continued.

"Is there even such a thing as the elixir of immortality?" they asked Shukracharya, who responded with a hard stare.

Back and forth, back and forth, to and fro, the literal tug of war went on and on, between the Devas and the Asuras, as the tired Vasuki supported them, most patiently. Although everyone was beginning to get exhausted beyond bearing, they continued with the churning. The Devas and Asuras were in it together. Being *Kashyapaih,* born from the great sage Kashyapa, they were siblings after all, and anxious to get to the nectar.

But, lo and behold, as the efforts continued, a marvelous, serene figure rose from the tumultuous depths. *Parama-adbhuta*, most spectacular, this was Dhanvantari, the divine physician. Strong and stout, *mahoraskah*, of a broad chest, he looked like the alpha lion. His polished ear loops made from pearls matched the radiance of his form. He donned yellow garments; his hair was well-oiled and his presence bore the promise of rejuvenation and good health.

His wrists were *valaya-bhushitah*, decorated with bangles, as he cradled a chalice filled to the brim with nectar in his long shapely hands, each finger sporting a precious ring. Some fingers were adorned with more than one ring. His very appearance was a living testament to the beauty of youth and glamor. Everyone knew in an instant that Dhanvantari was holding the elixir of life.

Truth be told, he was *bhagavatah-sākshāt-vishnoh-amsha-amsha-sambhavah,* a fraction of a fraction of none other than Lord Vishnu himself. No wonder, then, that his emergence brought about untold energy and joy to everyone present there. *Ayurveda-drika,* most conversant in the science of medicine, Dhanvantari was accorded the status of a Deva fit to receive oblations in *yajnas*, sacred fire offerings.

"O Kamale!" Vishnu addressed Lakshmi, putting his hand on hers, "you are an enchantress, and in Vaikuntha's palatial garden we'll create timeless moments."

The goddess's smile blossomed like a lotus in spring, and she couldn't muster the courage to look at Vishnu. For, she feared, she would simply lose herself completely in the vastness of his gaze that carried an infinite number of universes. Narayana was the perfect being. When it came to Him, even Dhanvantari's radiance, charm and appeal was no more than that of a firefly's in front of a billion suns.

"But, for now, O Devi," Vishnu continued, "I need you to wait for me in Vaikuntha. I have some unfinished business here—"

He stopped midway, as it sounded like a fight broke out at the site of the churning. *This is not fair! How could this be! We'll kill you!* There was a big commotion. This startled the Goddess and she looked in the direction of the brawl, but Vishnu gently tilted her chin to bring her attention back to him.

"What is going on, O Govinda?" Lakshmi said.

"You know how the Asuras go wild in celebrations!" Vishnu deflected. "I was saying, I needed to conclude the churning event and I'd like you to wait for me in Vaikuntha."

He summoned his splendid mount, Garuda, and sent Lakshmi back to Vaikuntha with their sage-sons, Chiklīta and Kardama.

The scuffle had turned into a full-on riot. Dhanvantari was standing in a corner at his wit's end, because the mighty Asuras had snatched the chalice of nectar from his hands, and they had declared unilaterally that they were going to have it first. They did not trust the Devas, and rightly so. For the Devas, too, had decided even before the churning started that they were going to drink the elixir all by themselves, and would not offer any to the Asuras. They believed that the Asuras were crude and selfish, and that if they became immortal, it would only do more harm than good.

Dhanvantari, Indra, the sages and the Devas rushed to Vishnu and pleaded for his immediate intervention.

"This will be the end of the Universe, O Purushottama," they said to Vishnu. "Please do something. Before Dhanvantari could bring the urn to you, the Asuras got away with it."

Vishnu told them that the Asuras were not the ones with the dishonorable intentions, as they never meant to consume the nectar by themselves—they just wanted to drink it first.

If anything, the truth was that the Devas, including Vishnu, never intended for the Asuras to partake of the nectar in the first place. This was precisely why Shiva refused to be a part of all this, because with a moral and conscientious compass, he would not support depriving the Asuras. But Vishnu knew that if the civilizations of the world had to evolve, the way of the Asuras could not be made immortal. They would destroy everything.

And so he launched a *vidveshna kritya*, a tantric spell of quarrelling, and soon the Asuras began fighting among themselves as to who would drink the nectar first. Shukracharya, their guru, tried to talk some sense into them but they weren't having any of it. Since Bali, their king, had already received Varuni, the maiden from the ocean, even he shouldn't get the first chug, they contended. This bought Vishnu some time, and when Vishnu gets time, Vishnu gets everything.

Anxiously and certain that the Asuras would either consume or spill the elixir, the Devas looked in the direction of the Asuras. And poof, Vishnu was gone. This led to a bit of a conundrum as no one expected Narayana to disappear right when they needed him.

"What's that?" someone shouted, pointing towards the site of the churning.

"Who's that?" another said.

There was a glorious form emerging from the ocean. The Devas forgot all about the missing Vishnu. This was a beautiful woman, a spectacle, a marvel.

They had thought that the churning was all but over, and yet out walked the most magnificent beauty.

She was *anirdeshyam,* no one could ascertain where she was from. *Utpala-shyamam,* she had the the deeply tanned complexion of a newly blooming dark lotus with an *unnasa-ānanam*, a beautiful raised nose between tender cheeks. With her body sculpted like a perfect hourglass, she was *adbhutam-prekshanīya,* a spectacular marvel in every sense of the word. Her ample bosom made her waist look rather slender.

Unable to hide their desire, the Asuras and Devas struggled to bring normalcy to their faces and in their loins. Her *nava-yauvana*, newly youthful form, a perfect harmony of chiseled curves, was so supple and firm at once that she had *nirvrtta-stana,* the only thing unagitated in that assembly were her breasts.

"Pick your jaws up off the floor and close your mouths," Brihaspati said to the Devas. "This must be some play of Vishnu. Stop being so foolish."

Her fragrance was so real that it enticed bees which began humming around her. The men felt the tinkling sound of her anklets in their heartstrings, as if she was plucking them every time she moved. She was somewhat frightened though, like a carefree doe suddenly surrounded by hyenas. *Udvigna-locanam*, with her anxious eyes, now she darted a glance here, and now there. It was not just a gaze, but *bhrū-vilāsa*, as if she engaged in some amorous play with her eyebrows. Her every glance pierced like arrows at the hearts of the Asuras.

At Brihaspati's counsel, the Devas looked the other way. They knew there was no escape otherwise.

As the jewels from her neck cascaded down and settled in the crevice of her bosom, every tiny clinking of her ornaments wove a serenade that transported the assembly to another planet. Some rays of the sun bounced off but most passed through her translucent drape, revealing just enough to drive the Asuras and Devas mad with desire. The only thing more flowing than her dress was her hair, all the way down to her waist. Each strand was as if a slithering cobra burying its fangs of lust and desire into the flesh of the spellbound Asuras, who just couldn't stop leering at her.

"You cannot trust the Devas," she counseled, moving towards Bali.

"Will you be mine?" Bali said. "I can do anything for you."

"You are all alike," she said with a toss of her head. "First you make promises, and then you conveniently forget."

"O most beautiful one!" Bali said. "Try me. I can do anything for you."

"Anything?"

"You name it."

"Can you give me the urn you are holding?" she asked, innocently.

Bali apologetically told her that the Asuras and Devas had equal right to the contents of the urn. Since it did not belong to him, he could not give it to her.

"See, that's what I meant," she said. "All men make promises they don't mean and can't keep."

"But, Devi," Bali cried, "I can even die for you. It's just that this drink needs to be distributed equally amongst us and the Devas."

As she moved a step closer, the king turned slightly, swaying the chalice away from her fearing she might somehow just take it. But she leaned forward a little, her sheer drape sliding down a bit, revealing her cleavage.

"What is it anyway?" she said sweetly, as tresses tumbled about her face. "I think you don't want to make me a part of your life. Otherwise, you would have asked me to distribute it for you."

This was Bali's tipping point—he lost all sense of discrimination and judgement. Surrendering to her extraordinary beauty, he told her that he trusted her with every fiber of his being. She remained so nonchalant and glib that within a few moments, Bali asked her to take the urn and carry out the distribution.

"Only on one condition, however" she pronounced.

"Anything for you, my love," Bali said.

"You are not allowed to question my strategy or manner of distribution."

"O *parama-sundari*," Bali said, "you can do no wrong."

The youthful beauty made two lines of the Devas and the Asuras. Shukracharya was doing a face-palm already, but knew that once Bali gave his word, he would not back out. The Asuras, too, knew that it was all over for them. Their king had fallen for a woman no one knew anything about and her intentions didn't seem noble at all. And so, one of the Asuras—Swabhanu—quietly escaped and sat amongst the Devas, between the sun and the moon.

Brihaspati whispered to Indra, solving the mystery. "This seductress is Vishnu," he said. "This is his Mohini *avatara*. But remain quiet."

The finest temptress, Mohini walked slightly bent, captivating the imagination of the Asuras with every step. She had not only extracted a promise out of them not to question her but simultaneously, all their sense too. They sat in their line like statues, watching her as she duped them with honeyed words every time it was their turn to have the nectar, instead giving the Devas the real elixir.

The Asuras knew something was not right, they felt it in their bones, but they only woke up to cruel reality when Vishnu discovered that the Asura Swabhanu cunningly got a sip by sitting in the row with the Devas. In a flash, Mohini turned into Vishnu. The eyes that were doe-like a moment ago were glowing embers now, and he lodged his discus in Swabhanu's neck, beheading him. Swabhanu continued to live as Rahu-Ketu, as he had already consumed the nectar. The moon, sitting next to him, got the last sip; the Asuras cried foul and launched a formidable attack.

"You can handle this now," Vishnu said to the assembly of Devas who, due to their newly gained immortality, were unconquerable. "I have to see about an important task that cannot be delayed any further."

The Devas valiantly fought the Asuras and would win, but for now, Narayana was back in Vaikuntha.

Mother Goddess was intrigued. She had many questions, but then she saw the cut on his finger he had gotten from releasing the discus. Nothing else mattered to her now, nothing in the Universe was important.

"I wonder of what use Dhanvantari is," she said while dressing his finger, "if he couldn't heal this."

"O Devi," Vishnu chuckled and said, "he only treats. I heal. And for now, I have important healing to do."

Vishnu held Lakshmi's tender wrist and had her take a seat on the throne. He summoned their youthful son-like sages, Chiklīta and Kardama.

"The emergence of any divine entity is incomplete unless they are accorded a place in the Vedas and *yajnas*," Vishnu spoke solemnly. "Sri is not just any goddess; she is one of the *mahavidyas*, a supreme goddess. Her sonic form will take thousands of years to complete because that is the natural evolution of wealth and prosperity. Good things take time. In her material form, she will be *anapagāminīm*, fluid like water, forever moving. Indeed, immanent in all forms of wealth, her utility will be in her liquidity. I ask both of you to invoke the next verse by performing a *yajna*, fire-offerings. *Jātaveda,* the sacrificial fire himself will purify and extend the offerings to my heart, Narayani."

"O Keshava! Hey Madhusudana," Lakshmi exclaimed with shyness and joy she couldn't hide. "How well you know me! You are the *veda, vedavida, avyangah*—the vedas themselves, the knower of vedas and faultless. It is true that as the inherent *sattva,* essence, of all wealth, it is in my nature to move, but when it comes to you, O Hrishikesha, I have no desire to go anywhere. You are my anchor. Wherever you are, I will accompany you."

And so it is to date. You may have seen pictures of Lakshmi where she's mostly standing. It's her nature to not be stable. But whenever she's shown next to Vishnu, she's always sitting by His feet. Wherever Vishnu is worshipped, Lakshmi stays. Vishnu represents wisdom and *nīti*, a moral framework, wealth stays there in the form of prosperity.

With the Divine Mother seated on the throne, Vishnu imparted the second verse of Sri Suktam to both Kardama and Chiklīta as they made fire-offerings in the *yajna*. These sages are acknowledged as the seers of this verse that contains one mantra. They chanted in unison:

तां म आवह जातवेदो लक्ष्मीमनपगामिनीम् ।
यस्यां हिरण्यं विन्देयं गामश्वं पुरुषानहम् ॥

tāṃ ma āvaha jātavedo lakṣmīmanapagāminīm ।
yasyāṃ hiraṇyaṃ vindeyaṃ gāmaśvaṃ puruṣānaham ॥

O Agni! Invoke for me the Goddess who will stay by my side and bless me so I may acquire material wealth of gold, cows, horses and attendants.

It was an extraordinary sight. Sri and Hari receiving offerings of the *yajna* to the chanting of the beautiful verse by the divine sages Chiklīta and Kardama; such oblations being taken out of a large fire-pit and offered to them by none other than Jātaveda, the personification of fire itself.

Vishnu reminded them that the invocation was being done for the welfare of the world, for the progressing humanity which was still in its nascent stages with *Homo sapiens* not being as evolved, and therefore, a minority back then.

"The time has come," Vishnu said, "to unlock the life-force of Sri Suktam. Wealth is dangerous in the hands of a dunce. Besides, while wealth may bring abundance, it does not mean prosperity. To experience lasting joy from material wealth requires not just detachment but an understanding of its inherent nature."

At Vishnu's instructions, Chiklīta and Kardama completed *purashcharana*, the rites of invocation, for the first two verses of Sri Suktam, and individually for each of the eight mantras contained in those verses. The entire process took three years at the end of which, having tasted the bliss of awakened mantras, the two sages wanted more, and thus approached Vishnu.

They said they were in constant bliss, as if they were *vayugamya*, floating, and they wanted to invoke the entire

Sri Suktam. Vishnu smiled at their longing, ignorance and audacity.

"My sons," Vishnu said. "Sri Suktam is not just a hymn. When complete, it's a living embodiment of your mother. It is supposed to be invoked gradually, by many sages, as humanity progresses. You can't just invoke the verses at your will and leisure, this must be done steadily and with permission."

"But permission from whom?" they said.

"From the Goddess herself!" Vishnu replied.

He went on to tell them that as the empress, since Sri Suktam was her own sonic form and as such carried all the attributes of the Goddess, the next two verses represented her heart and mind. And being an independent entity, she was entitled to make up her own mind and heart.

Mother Goddess intervened, smiling shyly, and said, "I belong to you, O Janardana. You are my heart and you are my mind. So, you decide for me."

"What you say is true, Subhage, bearer of good fortune," Vishnu said, "But you know that the foundations of the science of mantra and tantra have been laid by my beloved Shiva himself. I do not wish to circumvent them. But, Sri Suktam being your living sonic personification, you have the right to give permission to your sons if you wish for them to invoke the entire hymn."

Despite the maternal love the Goddess had for her sons, she was under no illusion that invoking the entire hymn was a mission that just two people could accomplish. She was well acquainted with her own power. It was clear to her that she could neither be so rash nor so attached that she granted her sons the approval for invoking the entire hymn. What if they fell ill and couldn't complete the task, how deformed would the nature of wealth then be in the world?

"Keshava," Mother Goddess spoke gently, "when I first emerged from the ocean, I was shy and instantly in love with you. The first verse was invoked in that vast gathering at the churning site. For the second verse, you had me sit down in Vaikuntha, and we received oblations. Can I now give consent that the next two verses be jointly invoked by Chiklīta and Kardama?"

"Of course, you can," Vishnu said. "But it's best if it comes from Shiva."

"But you just said that I could make up my own mind and give permission."

"Indeed, you can and you have done so," Vishnu affirmed. "But the final stamp of approval had best come from Shiva."

This confused the goddess and the sages a little. They felt Vishnu was being cryptic. But Vishnu was just being Vishnu. He was being democratic without bending the rules. He needed the goddess to have a say, but also be aware of the protocol and the ramifications of her choices.

"All pleasures and attainments, all growth and progress, O Ramā," Vishnu said, "carry in themselves the seeds of destruction. Whether that's transformation, transmutation, or transference, they are various aspects of destruction. And destruction is Shiva's domain. My advice would be to let Shiva participate in the invocation of your Suktam. Let the Mahayogi take the decision on whether Chiklīta and Kardama should invoke the next two verses, the entire remaining hymn, or no verses at all. He is most impartial. And trust me, He will not disappoint you. It's best to honor the Vedic tradition of mantra invocation."

Lakshmi saw the merit in Vishnu's concern and counsel. There was a real possibility that future generations would accuse Her, along with Vishnu, of partiality and the abuse of power, if she arbitrarily endorsed her sons for invoking further verses. And so she agreed, readily.

"So, what is your command now?" Chiklīta and Kardama asked.

"You must go to, who else but the greatest yogi, Shiva," Narayana said, as a smile escaped his lips. "Oh, and don't go empty-handed. Approach him with utmost humility like you would a guru."

"But, is it really that important to drop in on Shiva?" Chiklīta said. "This hymn is the sonic form of our mother—can we not just remain in your *sānnidhya*, company, and invoke the verses?"

Vishnu replied in the negative; he urged Chiklīta not to violate Vedic protocol. Chiklīta sought his forgiveness, and readily agreed to embark on the journey that would have far-reaching consequences for him.

With that, Vishnu sent them on a mission to understand the nuances of Sri Suktam and to invoke its next verse, if Shiva so willed.

अश्वपूर्वां रथमध्यां हस्तिनादप्रबोधिनीम् ।
श्रियं देवीमुपह्वये श्रीर्मा देवी जुषताम् ॥३॥

aśvapūrvāṃ rathamadhyāṃ hastinādaprabodhinīm ।
śriyaṃ devīmupahvaye śrīrmā devī juṣatām ॥ 3 ॥

In the threefold abode, namely the intelligence, vital air and the physical body, I exist in three ways, namely as a horse, elephant, and a chariot.

At the beginning of the meditation I produce a sound (nada) which resembles the neighing of a horse. When I enter the arterial duct, I produce a sound resembling the rattling of a chariot, and when I am inside the hollow within (the sushumna), I produce a sound resembling the trumpeting of an elephant. Yogins practising yoga comprehend me in these three ways.

The Rising of Kundalini

Verse 3

With the blessings of Lakshmi-Narayana, the sage brothers Chiklīta and Kardama began their journey to Kailasha, the abode of the Mahayogi. They didn't have Shiva's Nandi or Vishnu's Garuda to hasten their odyssey. Instead, they had to tread the arduous path, do the real walk. Not surprisingly, Vishnu wanted it that way because the journey of sadhana offers more power and insight than the actual success of it. He wanted his sons to embark on this expedition with a sense of responsibility, sincerity, and adventure, as opposed to entitlement.

Chanting holy names and the two verses of Sri Suktam, the brothers trekked up the difficult route. A few years had passed since the churning of the ocean, and Shiva was no longer in any camp near the site, but back in Kailasha. And everyone knew that if you wanted to see him, you had to go to him. He was not going to travel for anyone, except maybe Vishnu. No one, no matter how powerful or great, ever took offense at this quirk.

Such was the enigma of Shiva that he had the complete allegiance of millions of people belonging to all kinds of species. Whether it was the Devas, who lived a few hundred miles from Kailasha, predominantly in the upper region of the Himalayas, or the Asuras who lived thousands of miles away, closer to the coastal regions and on islands—they all revered him. In fact, they feared him for two chief reasons: one, his own tribe Rudra was vast and indomitable, and two, Vishnu never opposed Shiva or vice-versa.

Nobody could gauge the origins of the Mahayogi. He had just appeared mysteriously one day, in the woods of the Himalayas. For his devotees, he would sometimes recall and reveal his other reflections in parallel universes. In a way, Shiva was a rebel, a revolutionary, a yogi par excellence; but above all, he was a *tapasvin*. An austere ascetic who couldn't care less about power, fame, or the glory of being included in the Vedas. And yet there he was, in every major scripture. More than 70 hymns in the Rig Veda alone were dedicated to Shiva. In Yajurveda, a whole section of 11 *anuvakya*, chapters, with 121 mantras, known as *namakam*, was entirely dedicated to singing Shiva's glories. Its second part—*chamakam*—which primarily concerned itself with the devotees expressing their desires, had some 363 mantras. It holds just as intact today, and is collectively known as Sri Rudram. Over a period of time, as the Vedic era took hold of the Indian subcontinent and adjacent nations, there was no region that did not know of Shiva or hold him in deep reverence. And all because Shiva's straightforwardness, his impartial nature, had struck a deep chord with all species. By virtue of his own penance and powers, Shiva granted his followers boons of all kinds. His somewhat rebellious nature freed many who had been decreed against by the Devas, for whatever sins. Anyone who sought his refuge found his refuge.

And so, the sage brothers didn't mind the difficult journey. Although, Chiklīta did share with Kardama that he felt that if Lord Vishnu wished so, he could have easily given them permission to invoke the verses in Vaikuntha itself, rather than asking them to travel to Kailasha. When Kardama did not reply, Chiklīta naturally assumed that he was not interested in having this conversation; whereas in reality, Kardama had been so immersed in his inner world of devotion towards the divine hymn that he hadn't heard Chiklīta at all.

At any rate, the great Shiva himself—who was a total recluse and never involved himself in or meddled with anything that didn't concern him—was going to talk to them about Sri Suktam, Chiklīta thought. And that was much more than anyone could ever ask for. As they passed through various plains, hills, valleys and forests, they developed a deeper appreciation for the supreme ruler too, their own father, the phenomenal Vishnu. They were beginning to understand why material wealth was essential to progress. Not only did wealth provide for individuals, it also validated their existence, it seemed. This is how it was back then, and this is how it is today.

It took them several months to reach Kailasha, but finally their journey of nearly 2500 miles was over. The Himalayas took their breath away as they looked on at the mountain jewel, surrounded by smaller mountains. It was like a 24-carat solitaire with tiny baguettes studded on both sides. The giant mountains seemed to whisper of tales even more ancient than the era they already belonged to. Unlike the mount Kailasha of today, half a million years ago it was covered in dense forest, as groves of teak, deodar, sandalwood and many other trees filled the air with an intoxicating aroma.

Occasionally, sunlight filtering through the tall pines would cascade in radiant shards on the sage brothers, playing a game of hide and seek with the shadows below. At times, such shafts of light would illuminate patches of moss that intermittently carpeted the ground, in varying shades of green—from the soft hue of emerald, to the deep richness of jade.

They scaled the mountain where Shiva lived. None of his *ganas*, followers, stopped them, as soon as they heard that the brothers had been sent by Vishnu. The sage brothers were expecting to be extremely tired, but there was something magical about the place. The flora, the air, the ether, rejuvenated them with every step. They could understand, perhaps, why Shiva or his *ganas* never participated in the churning of the ocean. Forget the chalice of nectar, here every breath was as if it were filled with the elixir of immortality.

Part of the mountain had been cut flat, they discovered, as they reached the top. There was a raised stony platform covered by the hide of a lion while a *dhuni*, a live firepit with wood, had filled the air with fragrance as a log of sandalwood was smoldering with low flames. Next to the *dhuni* was planted a trident made from a metal they couldn't identify. A coat of ashes from the *dhuni* had settled on the trident, as if it hadn't been moved for days and weeks on end—which was quite possible as Shiva was known to go into deep samadhi for rather long periods. During such times, either Divine Mother, Uma herself, would tend to the *dhuni*, or when Shiva was in solitude, one of the *ganas* would do that for him.

On the platform was resting a *kapāla*, an inverted skull, cut out into the shape of a bowl—this was Shiva's waterpot. The

Mahayogi sat there, smeared in ash. He was wearing bracelets on his fair wrists, and armbands of rudraksha on his sculpted biceps. His matted locks were tied in a bun at the crown of his head, while his large forehead sported a *tripundra*, three horizontal lines.

The oddest thing that immediately stood out for the sage brothers was that Shiva was sitting under a giant banyan tree. Its branches reached out to one another, creating a sublime, if not mystical tapestry overhead. This was probably the only banyan tree in the whole of the Himalayas. It just didn't belong there, but then again, was there anything the great yogi could not manifest?

"How is my beloved Padmanabha?" Shiva said. Takshaka, the serpent around his neck, moved about a bit when he spoke.

Chiklīta and Kardama looked on speechless at the marvel that Shiva was. He was wearing loops in his ears made from the most purified mercury. As a beam of sunlight fell on it, it sparkled with an unearthly twinkle. Everything about him was divine: his broad chest, straight back, the wild abandon with which he sat unmoving in *padmasana*. The brothers performed full-length prostrations before the Mahayogi, and then a circumambulation, before sitting down at Shiva's indication.

"Lord Hrishikesha has sent an offering for you," Chiklīta said and reached into his bag. Both sage brothers then stood up in respect and offered a conch to Shiva, with great deference.

As soon as Shiva saw the conch, he gave a hearty laugh. He knew that this was Vishnu indicating something. And so it would be, a few thousand years later, Shiva would slay the demon Jalandhara and spread his ashes in the ocean. Those ashes would make their home in many conch shells, thereby forbidding Shiva from ever being offered libations with a conch.

"Well, now I know how he is," Shiva chuckled. "Playful as ever."

Chiklīta and Kardama sought the Mahayogi's guidance on invoking the remaining verses of Sri Suktam. In the same breath, they also mentioned that Mother Goddess, Lakshmi, had proposed that they could invoke two more verses, but that Lord Vishnu had said that only Shiva could grant permission on if, and how many passages of Sri Suktam, the two brothers could bring to life.

"Ah! Sadhana, Sri Suktam, the churning of the ocean… I see, I see," Shiva said, as if reminiscing. "Tell me O learned sages, what *dakshina,* offering, are you willing to make in return?"

"Anything you ask, O Mahadev!"

"Shiva does not ask for anything, but that doesn't mean that you won't have to give anything."

They couldn't understand exactly what the Mahayogi meant and they certainly were not expecting him to be cryptic like Vishnu. At any rate, they decided it was best not to press for explanations, as it might well be that Shiva was being straightforward and yet *they* couldn't understand him. The sage brothers sat there, with their hands folded.

"Permission granted to invoke the next two verses," Shiva broke the silence after a long pause. "I hereby initiate you into the third verse."

The Mahayogi removed the serpent coiled around his neck and laid it next to him. He then chanted the verse, out loud:

अश्वपूर्वां रथमध्यां हस्तिनादप्रबोधिनीम् ।
श्रियं देवीमुपह्वये श्रीर्मा देवी जुषताम् ॥

aśvapūrvāṃ rathamadhyāṃ hastinādaprabodhinīm ।
śriyaṃ devīmupahvaye śrīrmā devī juṣatāṃ ॥

The tall trees in the vicinity swayed, dispersing a waft of fragrance, while the leaves of the banyan tree fluttered, and fragments of snow still on the leaves came tumbling down. Some landed where Shiva was sitting, while many flakes disappeared a few feet above the *dhuni*. It was as if everything in nature was paying homage to Shiva.

He then relaxed from his posture, put one of his legs down and summoned the sage brothers closer. Putting his hands on each of their shoulders, he whispered the mantra again. Chiklīta received the instruction in his left ear while Kardama naturally took it in his right ear.

"There is a cave at the base of this mountain," Shiva said. "Park yourselves there and chant this verse in your mind every day, all the time. Step out once a day, either at dawn or dusk, for no more than one *muhūrta*, a period of 48 minutes. My *ganas* will provide you food once a day. Come back to me after three summers have passed."

Chiklīta and Kardama offered their obeisance and left, to carry out the instructions. With impeccable discipline and supreme concentration, they meditated on the verse by chanting it in their minds every waking moment. While invoking the first two verses had led to a rather devotional experience, the third verse felt like it was in another dimension. From the second year onwards, with each passing day, they felt as if their very bodies would melt away with the verses, and that like the reverberating sound of the hymn, they would disperse into thin air. If not under Shiva's instruction and tutelage, they might even have abandoned the pursuit midway.

By the time the three-year period ended, they were no longer just two sages trying to invoke a verse. Instead, they had become the very verse themselves. They had become one with the sound they had been meditating on. Shiva called them *mantramayi*, the final stage of a practitioner when he becomes one with the mantra.

"You can invoke the fourth verse anywhere," he said to them.

Delighted and grateful, they sought his leave so they could go back and invoke the fourth verse live, in front of the Mother Goddess, Lakshmi, their very own mother.

Shiva threw back his head and laughed. He then said, "Remember I asked you what you could give me in return and you had replied with, 'Anything'?"

Both nodded.

"Well, you have no Lakshmi to go back to. I need you to give up your attachment as your *dakshina*," Shiva said. "You have realized her *ananga*, formless, kundalini aspect. She lives in you. That's what the third verse is about. Two things are formless: *samriddhi*—prosperity, and *kāma*—desire. You cannot hold, touch, or feel either of those. There are physical objects and signs that may indicate their presence but on their own, they are formless."

Seeing the alarm on the sages' faces, particularly Chiklīta's, Shiva smiled and assured them that this was simply one of the stages of invocation; that for now, it was important to understand the other dimension of Sri Suktam—the inner dimension.

"The entire *samudra manthan*, churning of the ocean, is every living entity's inner struggle," Shiva continued. "The fight between opposing forces and voices of the mind is what *deva-asura sangrām*, the battle of Devas and Asuras, is. The whole process of awakening, after great inner churning, and the final triumph in the battle, is contained in the third verse."

Lord Shiva expounded for Chiklīta and Kardama the science of awakening one's primordial energy so one could rise above cyclical emotions and unleash the power of their superconscious. He also revealed to the sage brothers the six hidden mantras in the third verse and told them that there were a total of 53 mantras in the entirety of Sri Suktam. Each mantra capable of accomplishing the extraordinary.

Based on Lakshmi tantra, numerous other texts, and my own years of experience, too, I can tell you that this verse alone can help awaken in anyone their kundalini—with diligent practice, of course. And it reveals the esoteric meaning of the great churning of the ocean too.

The literal meaning of the verse is:

I invoke Sri, the resplendent Mother Divine who is the Goddess of prosperity, most gloriously accompanied by her retinue of horses in the front, chariots in the middle and

whose arrival is announced by the trumpeting of elephants.
May she come and bless me.

In Lakshmi Tantra, in her own words the Goddess says, *"I exist in three different ways. I exist as ashwa, horses, also as chariots, and I exist as the sound of the elephants. When I enter as a yogi's breath, in the first phase of the sadhana, the sound they experience is the sound of the neighing of horses. When I enter the middle stage of their breath, of their consciousness, they experience the sound of the rattling of wheels of the chariot. Towards the end, in their minds, they hear sounds as though elephants are trumpeting."* (Paraphrased)

When you embark on the journey of realizing yourself through yogic practices and meditation, in the beginning—if you see how horses run—it is a 'tap-tap-tap-tap' sound you hear within yourself. Once you settle into that rhythm, then emotions, thoughts, desires, temptations, unfulfilled cravings, and so on, will start to rattle your experience. So the middle phase in any sadhana is the most difficult phase. In the beginning you have the energy to say yes, I am going for it. In the middle, you start to question things, so it goes 'gad-gad-gad-gad'—a dull sound. Think of a chariot or a bullock cart moving on an unpaved road, pathway, or a village road. That's the middle sound.

And the third is the 'hhhmmmmm' sound, when the ringing of *anāhat nāda,* the unstruck flowing sound, starts. When you hear this in your heart, it is the most magical experience. It is like conches are blowing, elephants are trumpeting. When you are immersed in sadhana, you will hear distant sounds resonating right within you.

In the churning of the ocean, Uchchaishravas, the horse, came before Airavata, the elephant. Meanwhile, the churning itself was the chariot, the middle stage, the lifelong pursuit of carrying oneself across.

Presently, hearing the esoteric meaning of the third verse from the supreme teacher, Shiva, had a more profound effect on Kardama than on Chiklīta. Its impact was so deep that Kardama would go on to become an exceptional ascetic, completely immersed in devotion.

"I'm perfectly okay with the Mother Goddess being formless," Kardama said, in a calm voice. Like a placid Himalayan pond at night, there was not a ripple in his consciousness. His equanimity, his awakening, was so palpable that it stunned his brother who was suffering from anxiety and the pangs of separation. Chiklīta was distraught that he had no mother to go back to anymore.

"It baffles me, O Mahadev! Nothing is hidden from you," Chiklīta said. "Please enlighten us. We both emerged at the same time, chanted the same verses. I even invoked the first one on my own. We practiced the same routine in invoking the third verse and yet… Kardama has found supreme devotion and detachment in his heart, while I am heartbroken that I have lost my mother. How come? Why?"

It was a genuine question but with the third verse already invoked, Shiva had other plans for now.

कां सोस्मितां हिरण्यप्राकारामार्द्रां ज्वलन्तीं तृप्तां तर्पयन्तीम् ।
पद्मे स्थितां पद्मवर्णां तामिहोपह्वये श्रियम् ॥४॥

kāṃ sosmitāṃ hiraṇyaprākārāmārdrāṃ jvalantīṃ tṛptāṃ tarpayantīm ।
padme sthitāṃ padmavarṇāṃ tāmihopahvaye śriyam ॥ 4 ॥

I directly dissolve all the shortcomings of those who approach me and take refuge in me. I burn for ever in the deepest sphere of everybody's mind as the pure, impeccable reality illuminating the world with my rays.

I am filled with everlasting love for Hari and when pleased, I constantly shower gifts upon my devotees. I take spontaneous delight in the offerings of non-material objects. Sages, well versed in Vedic learning, envisaging me as the ever contented (goddess), attain to me who am the source of all knowledge, the transcendent and everlasting contentment full of nectar.

Molten Gold

Verse 4

"For now, just understand this," Shiva said. "The value of wealth is relative, and it is in scarcity. In the face of never-ending desires, even absolute abundance feels insufficient. And so in two places, Goddess in the form of Sri will live eternally: in the earth and in gold. Invoke her with the fourth verse for now. When you're done, I'll answer your question."

In his deep baritone, as if it were the rumbling of giant rocks, Shiva chanted the fourth verse of Sri Suktam.

कां सोस्मितां हिरण्यप्राकारामार्द्रां ज्वलन्तीं तृप्तां तर्पयन्तीम् ।
पद्मे स्थितां पद्मवर्णां तामिहोपह्वये श्रियम् ॥

kāṃsosmitāṃ hiraṇyaprākārāmārdrāṃ jvalantīṃ tṛptāṃ tarpayantīm ।
padme sthitāṃ padmavarṇāṃ tāmihopahvaye śriyam ॥

"O twin sages," Shiva said, "*kam-sosmitam*, smiling gently, the form of Lakshmi is like molten gold. She is *ardram*, she represents soft, fertile land. The Goddess Sri is *jvalantim*, radiating like fire. Because she is fire, she will illuminate everything, and will bring great warmth. But for the same reason that she's fire, her pursuit in her material form will totally consume men—it'll burn them up. She is also *triptam*, bringing deep satisfaction wherever she appears. And she is *tarpayantim*, the path to the fulfillment of all material desires. She will feed the entire world."

The great Mahayogi went on to tell the sage brothers that in the material world, Lakshmi will be the single most important enabler. No wonder, the sages had declared at the churning that she was everyone's *lakshya*, goal. Initiating them into the fourth verse, he once again drew the brothers close, put his left hand on Chiklīta's left shoulder and right hand on Kardama's right shoulder, and whispered the mantra in one go.

"Meditate on her as if she's made of gold," Shiva said, pointing to a snow laden peak where the setting sun had liberally painted the mountain golden. "That's her color."

"Go and chant in the cave, like the last time," he continued, "but every day, offer one thousand lotuses each. My *ganas* will arrange those lotuses for you each day. I will see you three summers hence."

The determined Chiklīta and the tranquil Kardama sat in searing *tapasya*, penance, performing an offering of one thousand lotuses daily. While both the brothers were exceptional *sadhakas*, after the invocation of the third verse, there was a marked difference between the two. Sadhana brought more ambition, even aggression, in Chiklīta while it made Kardama increasingly calm.

The only thing Chiklīta wanted by the end of the invocation of the fourth verse was to be able to go back to the physical form of Mother Goddess, whereas Kardama seemed mostly unaffected.

"That's because I have faith in Shiva's word," Kardama said. "He said this was just a stage, temporary, so it must be true. Besides, our father, our Ishta, asked us to approach the great

Mahayogi. So the question of any doubt in him doesn't arise. What is to happen will follow of its own."

Kardama's existence was a seamless sequence of blessed moments, each flowing into the next. He was liberated already, because he neither wanted nor expected anything from his sadhana. His sole motivation was to uphold the word of Lakshmi-Narayana and Shiva, his guru.

In contrast, Chiklīta felt waves of ambition, attachment, even envy. Persistent thoughts of surpassing Indra or being a powerful king lingered on in his consciousness. He repeatedly found himself being hit by bewilderment, as he had never imagined the possibility of having such thoughts, let alone wanting those things. He felt angry at himself for envying Kardama for his serenity and composure.

Chiklīta had tried speaking with his brother a few times but not only was it difficult for Kardama to understand his emotions, Kardama also wished to be quiet and remain immersed in his sadhana. Kardama wanted to honor the instruction of his guru with his heart, mind, and soul. The more Chiklīta meditated on Mother Goddess's golden form, the more he wanted gold in his life—which was rather strange because it was not like he had really seen the flamboyant life of Indra. But then again, he had been a witness to the affluence of Vishnu, whose opulent lifestyle was vastly different from the austere ways of Shiva. What Chiklīta couldn't wrap his head around was—how come he had none of these desires or feelings when he left Vaikuntha? Why him, why now?

Three years slipped by swiftly for Kardama, feeling as brief as three days; whereas for Chiklīta they unfolded as if it had been a tedious span of thirty years. But their efforts weren't fruitless, as a manifestation of Mother Goddess appeared before them, reaffirming Shiva's word that her disappearance would be temporary.

नमो नित्यानवद्याय जगत: सर्वहेतवे ।
ज्ञानाय निस्तरंगाय लक्ष्मीनारायणात्मने ॥

namo nityānavadyāya jagataḥ sarvahetave ।
jñānāya nistaraṅgāya lakṣmīnārāyaṇātmane ॥

I offer my obeisance to the eternally pure and unagitated Divine Mother who is the soul of Narayana, the foundation of existence, and absolute knowledge.

Thus they chanted with joy and in unison, welcoming the ever glorious *hiranyavarnam*, golden-hued, Mother Goddess. This was a prayer they had once heard Indra offer, and it had become their favorite one. Kardama offered the Goddess his prostrations, and then going back to his meditative posture, closed his eyes. He had gone beyond it all, his heart and mind steeped in fervent devotion, he desired nothing. He already felt the Divine Mother coursing through his very being, like blood through the veins.

Chiklīta, however, cried like a baby and held onto the Goddess's feet. She pulled him up and embraced him. The love and warmth she radiated soothed Chiklīta's parched soul. Yes, she was the goddess of wealth and opulence, but she was also his mother; and so her eyes brimmed with tears too. She understood how Chiklīta had been tormented with self-doubt and desires. She didn't need him to tell her how he was torn between conflicting voices, and plagued by ceaseless thoughts. She gently stroked his head and wiped a tear.

"Why mother, why?" Chiklīta cried. "Why did you disappear? And why couldn't I gain the serenity, calm and realization of Kardama? All I wanted to do was to bring your divine sonic form to life. Where did I go wrong?"

"Shhh…." Divine Mother said. "You are at *guru sthana*, your guru's abode. It is not my place to speak. Shiva alone will decide how much to reveal to you. I *had* to manifest here because you brought my form alive with my *suktam*, but also because I am a mother. I could not see you besieged with a broken heart and an ailing mind. Shiva will do what is right, he will do what's good for you."

She lovingly wiped his unrelenting tears with the hem of her silken drape, gently stroked his cheek, and disappeared. Chiklīta looked to his left and Kardama was still seated in *padmasana*. Motionless and silent, Kardama seemed like a sculpture of perfect equipoise and tranquility. *Was my vision real or was it my mind playing games*? Chiklīta thought. But undeniably, the air was filled with fragrance, it was full of love. He looked at the offering of that day, a pile of two thousand lotuses that lay in front of him. Both brothers had offered a thousand each. He felt as if he had woken up from a coma, trying to make sense of his surroundings.

Kardama arose as the sun was setting. In that twilight, the twin siblings came out of their cave and trekked up to Shiva's abode. It was dark. The transient dusk had fully surrendered to the sacred stillness of the night. The leaping and twirling flames from Shiva's blazing *dhuni* cast a mesmerizing glow on the Mahayogi's towering presence.

The sage brothers fell at Shiva's feet. Feeling overwhelmed, they prostrated themselves before him, giving him numerous reverential epithets such as *mahareta,* supreme nectar, *pashupati,* master of beings, *ugrateja,* fierce radiance, *kameshvara,* lord of desires, *mahatantra,* supreme tantra, *aghoranath,* master of the left-handed path, and many others.

"I am pleased with you," Shiva said. "But the remaining verses will be invoked by others over a period of time."

Kardama sat with his hands folded. Invoking more verses, however, was the last thing on Chiklīta's mind at the moment.

"Hey Neelakantha, have mercy on me, O Shambhu," he said. "The last three years have been exceedingly difficult for me. With your grace, Kardama and I have brought the fourth verse to life. And exactly as you said, I witnessed our Mother's manifestation again, but I feel less in control of my mind than ever before. All kinds of thoughts batter my consciousness, some of which I am even ashamed to mention. Why did the same sadhana have a completely different effect on my brother Kardama?"

"Chiklīta, be gentle with yourself," Shiva spoke with compassion. "While *bhagya*, fate, had a role to play in this, it is also because you underestimated the power of Vishnu's instructions. When he asked you to come to me for permission and initiation, you were unconvinced. Further, on your journey here, too, you could not persuade yourself to see me as your guru. That is why you questioned whether what Vishnu had advised was actually necessary. This was despite the fact that he had clearly told you to approach me like a disciple would approach a guru."

"O Mahadev!" Chiklīta couldn't hold back his tears. "Please forgive me. Must I pay such a huge price because of that one mistake, which I made out of ignorance?"

"Sometimes, mistakes are like seeds, O brilliant sage," Shiva said. "Even tiny ones can take deep root and grow tall."

The two brothers looked on, intrigued. The Mahayogi was quiet for a few moments.

"You see, Chiklīta," Shiva continued, "it was a stroke of luck, partially due to your *sanshya*—doubt—towards your guru, that you ended up sitting to my left and Kardama to my right. I initiated both of you at the same time. Since you were on my left, you got initiated into *vamachara*, the left-handed path of tantra designed to grant material gains and worldly wishes. Whereas Kardama was on my right, and he got initiated into *dakshinachara*, the right-handed path, the aim of which is liberation."

The Mahayogi went on to tell Chiklīta not to lose heart as he initiated him into the right-handed path and that it would take Chiklīta 12 more years before he could go back to Vaikuntha. Kardama would take up a place in the woods, to remain forever immersed in praying to the supreme lord.

"As a result of your penance, your origin, as well as your intent," Shiva said, "both of you have been accorded a place in the divine hymn itself."

And so it was that Kardama's name found a mention in the eleventh verse of Sri Suktam and Chiklīta's in the twelfth. It was again not a surprise when, in line with Kardama's intent, demeanor, initiation, and of course, destiny, the eleventh verse would be invoked by none other but the lord of liberation, Vishnu himself. The twelfth verse was invoked by an extraordinary sage—but it wasn't Vishnu.

"You are beyond blessed to have had the opportunity to invoke the first four verses," Shiva said, settling his gaze on Chiklīta. "Sri is the catalyst of the four *purusharthas*—endeavors of human existence, which are dharma, *artha, kama,* and *moksha* (moral duty, material wealth, fulfillment of desires, and emancipation.) By invoking the first four verses, you have already invoked all four. Kardama did not invoke the first one, dharma, so he will remain established in his body, pursuing the cause of dharma."

Across the four endeavors, there were 16 kinds of wealth, Shiva explained. Anyone mastering the 16 *richas*, verses, of Sri Suktam would end up acquiring untold wealth of all kinds, from all directions. The pacified Chiklīta and the ever serene Kardama beseeched Shiva to elaborate on the 16 kinds of wealth.

"Spread across dharma, they are: education, self-esteem, mental health and offspring or legacy," the Mahayogi replied. "In *artha*, they are: investments, business or vocation, houses as well as vehicles, and destiny. In *kama*, the four kinds of wealth are: a compatible life partner, physical pleasures, good health, and a steady source of income. And across *moksha*, the kinds of wealth are: spiritual knowledge, liberation, lifespan, and detachment, thus completing the 16 kinds."

As the fire crackled, embers glowed, and flames flickered, these were moments of deep silence and stillness in that incandescent dance of light. It felt as if the Universe held its breath in reverence to the discourse of the eternal yogi. His words were straightforward, but the enigma of his presence transcended the realms of mortal perception.

Other than their reverence for Shiva, the one thing the sage twins shared was the curiosity to see who would invoke the remaining 12 verses of Sri Suktam. A lot was still to be done. Who knew how long it would take?

चन्द्रां प्रभासां यशसा ज्वलन्तीं श्रियं लोके देवजुष्टामुदाराम् ।
तां पद्मिनीमीं शरणमहं प्रपद्येऽलक्ष्मीर्मे नश्यतां त्वां वृणे ॥५॥

candrāṃ prabhāsāṃ yaśasā jvalantīṃ śriyaṃ loke devajuṣṭāmudārām ।
tāṃ padminīmīṃ śaraṇamahaṃ prapadye'lakṣmīrme naśyatāṃ tvāṃ vṛṇe ॥ 5 ॥

My radiance is always and in all states superb. My brilliance, which is the ever active blissful consciousness, is always matchlessly bright. I am called Prabhasa by sages who are experts in the Tantra and Vedanta.

All the glorious fame acquired in this world on account of a person's scholarship or charity, etc., is a manifestation of myself. You should realize that it is I who is the recipient of all fame, brilliant power and opulence. Therefore the wise know me as Yaśasa.

In this world, all sublime revelation of great sages as well as all the capacities and activities of people in both the higher and lower stations of life come from me. Moreover, I bestow upon men their greatest aim in life, i.e. liberation, the shattering of bondage of life and death. Therefore the wise know me as Udara.

The Curse of the Sage

Verse 5

"Oh, Devala, my son, what have you done?" Asita Muni said, his voice quivering with angst and alarm. "The Gandharvas serve the Devas and are protected by none other than Shiva. This is not looking good."

Devala Muni was not an ordinary sage by any stretch of imagination. He was the son of the phenomenal scholar Asita Muni, and the grandson of the legendary sage Kashyapa, who was a longstanding honorary member of the governing council of the seven sages, also known as the *saptarishi*. What's more, Devala was a great *tapasvin* and savant himself. At a young age, his scholarship had been widely recognized, and as a result, he was the seer of 20 verses in the Rig Veda. To honor his father, he had Asita Muni acknowledged as a substitute seer for those verses. Between Devala, Asita and Kashyapa, their lineage had significant clout as they wielded profound political influence.

But what Devala Muni had caused today was not a political issue that could be remedied by pulling some strings. No, not at all. Instead, using the power of his penance, he had cursed a Gandharva. Gandharvas were the celestial musicians, even entertainers, for Devas, the gods; they had a sort of free reign in the name of entertainment, arts and comedy. Most did not approve of the conduct and mannerisms of the Gandharvas, as under Shiva's protection and the Devas' patronage, many of them had become increasingly arrogant and conceited.

Earlier that evening when Devala Muni was offering his libations, a Gandharva was frolicking in the river in the company of stunning damsels. Proud of his striking visage and golden voice that could rival the sweetest of songbirds, he was having a wild celebration. Alternating between loud singing and joking, the group would stop to sip wine and eat berries, before resuming their exuberant play.

This disturbed Devala, but he had come for his prayers and as such simply wanted to mind his own business. The Gandharva showed no respect for the presence of the sage, which, while awful, was not illegal. The disturbance escalated in no time, when the Gandharva—known as Huhu—pulled Devala's leg and dragged him into the deep end of the river. Seeing the radiant *muni* offer libations, most Gandharvas would have moved to another location, but not Huhu. Instead, he not only stayed back, but pranked the sage.

Thinking he was snagged by a crocodile, Devala Muni was particularly alarmed. But as soon as he bobbed his head above water and saw Huhu come up to bellow with laughter, he was beside himself.

Devala dipped his hand in the river and collecting a palmful of water, he uttered, "Get lost, you despicable scoundrel, be born a crocodile." And he splashed the water at the Gandharva. The celestial women disappeared immediately. The livid sage walked out of the river, Huhu behind him.

"Please forgive me," Huhu said, clasping his feet. "I made a terrible blunder in ignorance—"

"Ignorance!" Devala thundered. "Arrogance! It was your arrogance. Now sing all you like as a crocodile."

When Huhu repeatedly begged for mercy, Devala finally relented and told him that after a long time, he would be redeemed by Lord Vishnu. Until then however, he would live the life of a crocodile with its innate tendencies. Huhu asked if Shiva could expedite his redemption, in response to which Devala reminded him that Shiva would never slay a Gandharva. The entire tribe of Gandharvas had pledged their allegiance to Shiva, and they were under his protection. Therefore, no matter the reason, Shiva would not help Huhu get rid of the body of the crocodile by killing him. Accepting his fate, Huhu prostrated before the sage; that was his last prostration as a Gandharva as he soon found himself belly-crawling into the river and then onto the other bank.

When Devala reached home, he narrated the story to his father, Asita Muni, who expressed deep concern. The *muni* concluded that Devala, too, had acted in haste and rage, even arrogance. At first Devala tried to argue that he had cast that curse on Huhu because he had been interrupted in the middle of his sacred prayers. But soon he saw his father's perspective—of what use was Devala's penance and wisdom, if he didn't have the forbearance of a sage? To be patient and forgiving was the right choice according to Asita, particularly considering the fact that Huhu was already sporting in the river when Devala reached there. He said that Devala should have gone to a different spot.

"This will have far reaching repercussions," Asita Muni declared.

"What kind?" Devala was now beginning to get rather concerned.

"There was no need to bother Vishnu," Asita said. "Huhu would have eventually died as a crocodile to be reborn a Gandharva, but by saying Vishnu would redeem him, you have involved a third player. After all, Vishnu would not slay the crocodile without a reason. Further, Huhu as a crocodile lives far away from Vaikuntha, the domicile of Vishnu."

Asita looked away for a few minutes, as if peering deep into the future, while Devala stood with his head bowed in dead silence. "You see, my son," Asita Muni finally continued, "I can reveal exactly what's going to happen. Huhu has already forgotten that he was once a mellifluous Gandharva who melted stones and rocks with this voice. As a crocodile, he is going to attack a devotee of Vishnu who will call out to Him. Vishnu will come to save his devotee, and he will slay the crocodile with his discus. This is not going to sit well with Mother Goddess, Sri. As it is, brahmins have not done much to propitiate her."

"But why won't it sit well with her?" Devala asked, completely intrigued.

"Because every time Vishnu launches his discus, it slits his finger causing blood to ooze out. That injury takes a while to heal. Mother Goddess finds it unbearable that the ever benevolent and tender Lord Vishnu is subjected to that pain, especially in this case where events aren't arising out of the natural order of things, but due to a curse by a young sage who couldn't control his emotions. And to express her disapproval and displeasure, She walks away from the offender. In other words, our future generations will be bereft of all material wealth, success, and comforts."

Devala fell at his father's feet, realizing that the consequences of his blunder extended far beyond the boundaries of his understanding. But you cannot undo time, you cannot undo words.

Asita Muni's foresight was as impeccable as his insight. Several years later, while drinking water in the river, an elephant was grabbed by a crocodile—none other than Huhu. In deep pain, the elephant called out to Vishnu; seeing his plight, Vishnu descended to earth on his mount, Garuda, and launched his discus at the crocodile, slaying it instantly. Exactly as predicted by Asita Muni, the slim and tender index finger of Vishnu was nicked by the discus and upon his return, Mother Goddess found Devala to be the real culprit.

But in the present, since Asita Muni had already foreseen these events, he quickly left his wife, Ekaparna, and his son, to meet his father Kashyapa Muni.

"It is tricky, no doubt," Kashyapa Muni said. He had a soft spot for his grandson, Devala. "But, now is the time that Ekaparna's penance will also bear fruit."

Ekaparna had been a staunch *tapasvin* and a devotee of the Supreme Goddess, Durga. In another lifetime, when the Goddess herself had done searing penance to attain Shiva, she had subsisted on just dried leaves, *parna*, and eventually even gave those up. For such extreme *tapasya*, austere practice, she was given the name Aparna, the one who lived on not even leaves.

Asita Muni's wife, as part of her upbringing, had performed hard penance unknown to mankind by subsisting on just one leaf a day. Pleased by her devotion and determination, Ma Durga Herself had given her the epithet Ekaparna—she who survived on one leaf. Kashyapa knew that now was the time to use that card. He advised Asita Muni to meet Vishnu, and specifically ask for a tangible way to invoke Mother Goddess in the form of Sri, so Her benevolence and benediction be always upon their entire clan.

Without letting another moment slide, Asita Muni left for Vaikuntha.

"What a pleasant surprise!" Vishnu said smilingly, as soon as he saw the sage.

"O Lord Madhusudana," the sage said, "your devotees love your smile, but it worries me. This smile tells me not only that you know what has transpired, but also what calamity may fall on my lineage if you don't give me a way out. Please tell me how I may propitiate the Goddess and take a rain check on the misfortune."

Vishnu chuckled and said, "You couldn't have come at a better time. She is being revealed to the world, gradually, after the great churning of the ocean. Our sons have invoked the first four verses of her sonic form, known as Sri Suktam. It is about time that learned sages such as yourself got access to it. Just bring to life the fifth verse, and she will be delighted with you."

And so, Lord Vishnu imparted the fifth verse directly to Asita Muni.

चन्द्रां प्रभासां यशसा ज्वलन्तीं श्रियं लोके देवजुष्टामुदाराम् ।
तां पद्मिनीमीं शरणमहं प्रपद्येऽलक्ष्मीर्मे नश्यतां त्वां वृणे ॥

candrāṃ prabhāsāṃ yaśasā jvalantīṃ śriyaṃ loke devajuṣṭāmudārām ।
tāṃ padminīmīṃ śaraṇamahaṃ prapadye'lakṣmīrme naśyatāṃ tvāṃ vṛṇe ॥

Asita Muni invoked the verse and the eight mantras contained in this verse with single-minded focus and unrelenting devotion, praying to the Goddess to save him from any kind of misfortune.

"Actions cannot be without consequences, O Sage," Mother Goddess spoke, when she appeared. "But I am delighted with you. And so your *gotra*, lineage, started by your father, will survive eons and beyond. However, it will also be diverse and no longer restricted to only brahmins. That will be a blessing in disguise."

And so, descendants of Kashyapa spread throughout India and took important posts in administration, governance, defence, and later, agriculture and fisheries.

Such was the impact of his sadhana and scholarship that of the numerous sages who existed, both Asita and Devala not only found a mention in the Bhagavad Gita, but it was in the same verse that Vyasa is mentioned. Arjuna says to Krishna:

आहुस्त्वामृषय: सर्वे देवर्षिर्नारदस्तथा ।
असितो देवलो व्यास: स्वयं चैव ब्रवीषि मे ॥

āhustvāmṛiṣayaḥ sarve devarṣirnāradastathā ।
asito devalo vyāsaḥ svayaṃ caiva bravīṣi me ॥ BG 10:13 ॥

"Oh Krishna, everybody says you are God. Certainly Veda Vyasa himself says this, as well as Asita rishi, and Devala rishi. They have all declared that you are God."

Descendants of Asita Muni remained ardent worshippers of Vishnu and his consort. In fact, according to Bhagavata Purana, Asita Muni was the first one who declared baby Krishna as God. In Rig Veda, there are about 20 hymns where Devala Rishi is the seer and Asita Muni is the substitute sage of those verses. After the aforesaid major incident, Devala did not want to be acknowledged as the seer of those verses. Instead, he wished that those 20 verses be attributed to his father alone. But at his grandfather's bidding and with some clever work from Narada, both Devala and Asita came to be recognized as the seers of those verses.

For now, the narrative had to continue moving. Out of the sixteen verses, only five were invoked thus far. The sixth verse had to be brought to life by not just any sage, but someone who had a say in creation itself. In our lives, there are *shadripu*, six formidable enemies to one's spiritual progress. They all become strong when wealth, in the form of power, fortune or material gains, ends up in the hands of a non-deserving recipient. They are *kama, krodha, lobha, moha, mada* and *matsarya*—lust, anger, greed, attachment, false pride, and envy, respectively.

The sixth verse of the Sri Suktam must bring wealth to the seeker in a manner that would generate feelings of empathy, philanthropy, goodness and compassion. And so, Vishnu knew that he would have to get involved. Not only that, he would need to get someone very significant to do the job. Above all, he knew he would need to manifest the right conditions in his unique manner—in other words, Vishnu *leela*.

आदित्यवर्णे तपसोऽधिजातो वनस्पतिस्तव वृक्षोऽथ बिल्वः ।
तस्य फलानि तपसानुदन्तु मायान्तरायाश्च बाह्या अलक्ष्मीः ॥६॥

ādityavarṇe tapaso'dhijāto vanaspatistava vṛkṣo'tha bilvaḥ ।
tasya phalāni tapasānudantu māyāntarāyāśca bāhyā alakṣmīḥ ॥ 6 ॥

I alone make the sun brilliant with luminosity, illustriousness and beauty. Present in the sun as the essence of sound, embodying the divine Vedas, I reveal all objects of cognition, even those belonging to the past and to future. I am the eternal eye, vision, of the ancestors, of celestial beings and of human beings.

My sound-body is the subtle flame of pranava and resembles the continuing resonance of a ringing bell like a flow of oil. He who has realized Brahman will soon recognize my presence in pranava and I, consisting of sound, come together with all sounds produced from the aditya sound (i.e. pranava). The sages are familiar with all these various significations of my name Adityavarna.

The Haihaya Dynasty

Verse 6

Today was one of those routine visits by Indra and no one could have imagined that it would lead to the beginning of a whole new dynasty. At the great churning of the ocean from which Ma Lakshmi had emerged, there was another magnificent creature that had arisen: the fine stallion Uchchaihshravas. While Lakshmi had taken Vishnu as her consort, Indra—the chief of Amaravati where the Devas lived—was given Uchchaihshravas as a tribute. In fact, Indra had so taken a liking to this horse that he had staked a claim to it before anyone else could find their voice.

Although this was a long time ago, Indra still hadn't grown tired of Uchchaihshravas—which was rather unusual for someone like him, as Indra was a charmer, even a philanderer, and always sought variety in everything. But he had been so enamored and impressed by Uchchaihshravas that he even got him a mention in the Vedas. Even the chant of auspiciousness, Svastivachana, now included an acknowledgement of the stallion, at Indra's insistence. He could never admire the steed enough and he wasn't to be blamed, because Uchchaihshravas was truly special. And why not, as in some regards he was a sibling of Lakshmi, as both emerged at the time of Samudra Manthan.

That day, Lord Vishnu and Ma Lakshmi were already sitting out in the beautiful morning winter sun. The immaculately done garden was dotted with *parijata*, night-jasmine trees, *kadamba,* burflower trees, gardenia and fig trees. Autumn had just given way to winter and the foliage on some of the trees was still tender. Here and there, petals of some flowers, notably lavender, jasmine, rose, and leaves of some of the trees lay randomly on the plush bed of grass. Indra dismounted the horse and moved close to a tree to tether it, but Vishnu indicated that the stallion could be let loose.

A special seat was arranged for Indra, and after exchanging pleasantries, Vishnu started narrating an incident from a bygone era—when Uchchaihshravas walked slowly and sat close to Lakshmi. Its snow-white coat glistening in the sunlight highlighted every ripple of muscle beneath. Uchchaihshravas' ears fluttered occasionally, as if in tune with the breeze, like a dance only they shared. And out of its wide innocent eyes, it cast a serene glance at Lakshmi. The horse epitomized elegance.

Somewhat spellbound, Lakshmi began patting Uchchaihshravas. She completely ignored Vishnu, who had already called out to her a couple of times. It was not on purpose. Engrossed in her own world, she didn't realize that both Indra and Vishnu felt slighted. Lost in thought, Lakshmi was in a long and silent dialog with her sibling, the stallion. *I have never quite seen anyone as beautiful as you. O Uchchaihshravas, you are the finest of all horses ever born.*

Vishnu looked in the direction of Indra and then Lakshmi. He expected the Divine Mother to participate in their conversation, to answer his question, but she was completely lost in admiration of Uchchaihshravas. Vishnu had never seen

Lakshmi like that. It was a first. A fleeting shade of disapproval crossed his face, as he became still for a moment. Whether it was just his divine play or history in the making, it was an enigma for anyone to fathom.

"Since you like this horse so much," Vishnu said with a tinge of anger in his voice, "may you turn into a mare." This completely startled Lakshmi. She had never seen an ounce of anger in Vishnu, ever. She couldn't believe that the ever smiling Vishnu could speak in a tone like that to anyone, let alone utter a curse at *her*. Indra, too, was taken aback. Excusing himself immediately, he rode away. He believed it must be Vishnu's *leela* to articulate such words.

And Indra's guess was not untrue either. For Lakshmi would now take birth as a mare on earth and that would be the start of a marvelous dynasty known as the Haihayas. The most valiant Haihaya king was Kartavirya Arjuna, who was also known as Sahasrabahu—for he possessed the power of one thousand arms, and defeated the mightiest of kings, including Ravana. The Haihayas founded the magnificent city of Mahishmati (in present day Madhya Pradesh) on the banks of river Narmada.

It was therefore no surprise that one of the kings of this dynasty, known as Muchukunda, would be an ancestor of Lord Rama, who in turn was an incarnation of Vishnu, and suffered pangs of separation in that *avatara* as his consort, Ma Sita, would be abducted by Ravana. Rama and Sita would be separated for a period of 13 months. The ever free and unbound Vishnu had agreed to abide by karmic laws since, as Rama, he took birth in human form. There were other reasons for the temporary separation of Rama and Sita, and Vishnu's curse today was one of them.

For now, a different story was unfolding in Vaikuntha as Ma Lakshmi entreated Vishnu to withdraw his curse.

"Uchchaihshravas is my brother and I was just happy to see him. I meant no disrespect to you or our guest," Lakshmi said. "I know you would never just curse me like that. Whatever the reason, can that destiny not be fulfilled in any other way?"

"O innocent one," Vishnu said, holding the hand of the goddess. "You are an indispensable spoke in the wheel of time. I ask you to trust me at this stage. You alone are capable of playing this role."

Vishnu told her that the best way to hasten the entire process was by invoking Shiva. And he said that in order not to compromise the sanctity of the sadhana—since Lakshmi was a consort of Vishnu—it was better if Brahma advised her on the process of worship.

Without another moment's delay, she took leave of Vishnu and immediately left for Brahma's abode. The quiet and patient Brahma heard the entire episode and advised Lakshmi to offer ten thousand *bilva* fruit offerings to Shiva every day, and to keep doing this until Shiva appeared. Intrigued, Lakshmi asked the significance of offering *bilva* fruits, as sourcing ten thousand of them every day was going to be a difficult task.

"That's because you are Vishnu's consort," Brahma said, "and I recommend that you invoke Shiva with your feminine energy, and not merely as a devotee."

"With *bilva* fruit?"

"Yes," replied Brahma, and narrated the story of why the *bilva* fruit is dear to Shiva.

"Ages ago, long before the churning of the ocean, Mother Goddess Parvati, the supreme energy, was once playing with *yoginis*, her companion energies, when beads of sweat broke out on her forehead and they dropped to the ground. The two *yoginis*, Jaya and Vijaya, saw this uncommon occurrence, and knew something divine would come about. At the place where those drops of sweat fell, tiny saplings grew, and eventually turned into trees that bore fruit. They brought the fruit to the Goddess's attention who named them *bilva*, for their saplings pierced the ground to grow. She offered those *bilva* fruits to Shiva. When Shiva got to know the origin of the fruit, he took a special liking to them as, since they were born of the Goddess's sweat, they were like her—why, their—offspring. Anything born of sweat is classified as *svedaja.*"

"So you must offer *bilva* fruits to Shiva," Brahma said, and also bestowed a sacred mantra to Lakshmi.

Heeding the advice, day in, day out, she offered 10,000 *bilva* fruits to Shiva on a daily basis—except for one day when she ran out of the fruit with still two more offerings to go. Not wanting to leave her sadhana midway, she figured that the only other thing she could offer as a woman, a mother, a consort, or as a *sadhika*, was to cut her own body parts and to offer those to Shiva. And so, she grabbed a nearby knife with the intention of presenting her breasts as the last two offerings.

Shiva immediately appeared in his *ardhanarishvara* form, before Lakshmi could act on that thought. What a sight it was. The camphor-complexioned, perfectly sculpted body, wearing a tiger-skin, with one half of his body as the primal Goddess covered in an intricately woven cloth and bedecked with jewelry, and the other half as a masculine representation. Shiva spoke gently and told Sri that the only way she could be relieved of this curse was if she bore a son. Lakshmi expressed in great alarm that the only one in the three worlds she could ever be intimate with was Vishnu.

Shiva reassured her, "O Devi, daughter of the Ocean, drop your worries. I will send you Vishnu, the Lord of the world. He will come to you in the shape of a horse, to satisfy your desires. Madhusudana, the Deva of all Devas, will be passionately attached to you, as a horse. And you will go back to Vaikuntha as soon as you beget a son."

Lord Vishnu then, in his incarnation as Hayagriva—where he assumed a human body with a horse head—copulated with the mare that was Lakshmi, and started the Haihaya dynasty.

Upon fulfillment of the word given by Shiva, Lakshmi decided that she must first meet Brahma and express her gratitude for the guidance he had given her, before going back to Vaikuntha. But much to her surprise, Brahma began praising *her* instead.

"You are not just Lakshmi, you are Mother Divine, you are the Goddess, you are Parvati. There is no difference. You are the origin, end, and the sum total of all feminine energy. All wealth, prosperity and opulence are from you alone."

"When you appeared from the ocean," he continued, "along with your physical form, your sonic form, by way of Sri Suktam, too had emerged. Allow me, O Goddess, to sing your glories and bring to life the sixth verse of the powerful hymn."

And offering resplendent jewels, vermilion, turmeric, a large feast of most marvelous delicacies, sweet and savory, he seated the Goddess on a throne and chanted the sixth verse of Sri Suktam:

आदित्यवर्णे तपसोऽधिजातो वनस्पतिस्तव वृक्षोऽथ बिल्वः ।
तस्य फलानि तपसानुदन्तु मायान्तरायाश्च बाह्या अलक्ष्मीः ॥

ādityavarṇe tapaso'dhijāto vanaspatistava vṛkṣo'tha bilvaḥ ।
tasya phalāni tapasānudantu māyāntarāyāśca bāhyā alakṣmīḥ ॥

O splendid and dazzling Goddess, as a result of thy glories and penance have the sacred plants like bilva *come into existence. May the fruits of (such penance) destroy all inauspiciousness arising out of my impure thoughts and ignorant actions.*

Brahma, *hiranyagarbha*, the golden egg himself, prayed with much intensity as an ardent seeker, and invoked this mighty verse that brings confidence, good luck, and purity of mind to anyone who chants this verse.

उपैतु मां देवसखः कीर्तिश्च मणिना सह ।
प्रादुर्भूतोऽस्मि राष्ट्रेऽस्मिन् कीर्तिमृद्धिं ददातु मे ॥७॥

upaitu māṃ devasakhaḥ kīrtiśca maṇinā saha ।
prādurbhūto'smi rāṣṭre'smin kīrtimṛddhiṃ dadātu me ॥ 7 ॥

I spread my luminous rays all over this universe. I gradually manifest as sonic creation. Resting on the petals of each chakras, I slowly soar up along with the air, the friend of gods and with the gem, the basic fire and finally attain the state of emancipation. Hence the wise sages praise me as Kirti.

I flourish through Vishnu's attributes; I make the yogins happy. I gradually expand myself over all the petals of the lotuses of the yogin's yogic body, coming out of the lotus called root plexus, mulaadhara, and finally achieve the absolute state of expansion. Hence in ancient times yogins called me Riddhi, the brilliance of yoga.

The Clan of Maharishi Bhrigu

Verse 7

The seventh verse of Sri Suktam was invoked by Mrikanda Rishi. To really understand why he propitiated Mother Goddess with this verse, we have to go back to one of the most iconic sages of ancient times—Maharishi Bhrigu, the founder of the clan of present-day Bhargava brahmins.

With the power of his penance and purity, Bhrigu had gained unrestricted access to the abodes of the trinity of Brahma, Vishnu, and Shiva. He knew that any one of the trinity could grant powers and boons to their devotees, which they did routinely. But, who was the most forgiving? After all, mistakes were bound to happen, and if a practitioner made a grave mistake, would they be pardoned? Bhrigu thought, *If you cast a stone at a tree laden with fruits, it gives you back a fruit. What if devotees hurt their* ishta, *what will they get in return?*

It might have seemed like a random thought, when in reality it was anything but. The awakened sage understood that only the most forgiving of them was truly fit to be the ruler of the world. For, a good king must know when to be firm and when to be compassionate. This was the only way humanity was going to progress, he thought. He sincerely wanted to know who among the three was *bhakta-vatsala,* the one who has the most love for his devotees.

To discover the truth, Bhrigu decided to travel to all three Lords in his *sukshma sharira*, astral body. That would be the fastest way, he believed. In his mind's eye, he saw Brahma deep in dhyana. Bhrigu tried to wake up Brahma, without any success. Going to Shiva turned out even worse, as he ended up evoking the ire of the Mahayogi by disturbing him; he thanked his lucky stars that he'd only visited Shiva in his astral body, which helped him escape catastrophe. When Bhrigu approached Vishnu, he found him to be the most patient and welcoming.

"I must visit Vishnu in my physical body to validate my conclusion," he thought. The timing was perfect too, since during the harsh winters in the upper regions of Bharatvarsha, the vast Indian subcontinent, Vishnu spent his time in Kshirasagara. Although literally 'the ocean of milk', Kshirasagara was a pristine island in the coastal region of southwest India, where the sand was the color of cow's milk. This summer dwelling of Lakshmi-Narayana was a world of affluence in its own right.

Bhrigu had been in sadhana on *Raivata Parvata*, present day mountains of Girinar in Gujarat, when he decided to travel to Lord Vishnu in person. As it were, Kshirasagara was not far from there, and particularly with the resources and *siddhis* of Bhrigu, it was even closer.

Kshirasagara was no less than Vaikuntha. In a way it *was* Vaikuntha, a place devoid of sadness, the abode of Vishnu. The ever benevolent Narayana was not someone who interfered in the workings of nature, but one step into Kshirasagara and even a sightless person could tell that there was hardly anything natural about this place. It was full of nature all right, but to have plush gardens, palm trees, orchards, and diverse flora and fauna right next to the sandy ocean was a vista unseen elsewhere.

Bhrigu entered the main gates, where he was treated with utmost respect and let in without any check, for everyone knew Bhrigu. At a distance, the sun was shimmering over the tranquil waters of the ocean. It was as if all harmony in the cosmos had found its reflection in this realm of serene beauty. The great sage walked through the pathways dotted with flowers of various hues, while peacocks with unearthly plumage roamed freely. Koels were singing from various trees, while the deer played around, fearlessly. It was as if he had stepped into another era, another planet in a different galaxy.

At its heart, positioned most resplendently, was the divine palace of Lord Vishnu. Bhrigu spoke for a brief moment with Jay and Vijay, the main gatekeepers of the palace, and headed directly to the private chamber of Vishnu, where he was stopped by Lakshmi.

"He is in *vishrāma*, rest, Bhrigu," Mother Goddess said. "While I cherish your desire to meet Him, now is not an opportune time."

Bhrigu, however, was drunk on the power of his scholarship. The fact that he had unrestricted access to the holy trinity should have brought him a greater sense of responsibility. Instead, he felt entitled.

"I haven't come to meet you," Bhrigu replied, somewhat flippantly. "I have come to meet my Lord Narayana."

"You speak well, Bhrigu," the Goddess spoke softly. "Yet, the path lies through me. At present, the Lord is in serene repose, and I stand sentinel, entrusted with the solemn duty of safeguarding his interests. You must wait."

Ignoring her instructions, Sage Bhrigu rushed in and immediately slammed his foot on the sleeping Lord Vishnu's chest.

Startled, Lord Narayana woke up; seeing his devotee he smiled and asked, "O Bhrigu, what's the rush?" Bhrigu fell at his feet and said, "Please forgive me, O Lord! I have made a terrible mistake. I was just testing who is the God most fit to be worshiped by devotees when they need something… and you are the most gentle and compassionate of all!"

In that precise moment, Vishnu disappeared. He knew there would be fallout he did not want to be a part of. On the one hand was his own energy, his consort, and on the other an exceptional sage, his devotee. It was best to leave these two to figure it out for themselves, he thought.

It all happened too rapidly, before Lakshmi could do anything. Humiliated and angry that someone could do that to Vishnu, her delightful feminine presence transformed into a tempest of rage. She knitted her brows, her eyes full of ire, and her wrath, only too palpable.

"You hit him, Bhrigu!" she roared like a wounded lioness. "This is unpardonable. From this moment on, my mercy shall forsake you forever. You and your clan, all your descendants, will have to do without me."

Bhrigu stood there dumbfounded, as the Goddess of opulence deprived him and his entire future generations of brahmins of any wealth.

"Henceforth, your survival rests solely on your wisdom, for my grace shall be but a mere shadow, a fleeting memory in your future," She continued. "I will go to kshatriyas, merchants and landowners, but I will not come to you."

Undeterred by this extraordinary curse, composing himself, Bhrigu said, "I seek your forgiveness for what I did; but you underestimate the strength of my bond with Lord Vishnu. It may seem to you that blessing my progeny with wealth is in your hands, but with all due respect, I disagree. I am going to create a spell so powerful that you will be unable to resist the attraction."

"It seems that you speak in ignorance, Bhrigu," Lakshmi said. "I am beyond any spells."

"I am going to create a powerful scripture capable of foretelling anyone's future," Bhrigu responded. "People will make a material offering to acquire a reading from it."

And so he created the Bhrigu Samhita, which became the mainstay and foundation of astrology. It so transpired that those Brahmins who knew astrology fared better off in their material lives than those who didn't. Eventually, astrology went on to become a *vedanga*, a limb of the Vedas.

In due course, the sage Bhrigu became a father—his son was called Mrikanda. Since Mrikanda was born of Bhrigu's *tapas*, penance, he had the deep samskaras of self-awakening and realization. He figured out, quite early on, that his father's quarrel with Ma Lakshmi was not only avoidable but inappropriate too. After all, she was a part of Vishnu. He went on to placate and invoke Mother Goddess through the seventh verse of Sri Suktam:

उपैतु मां देवसखः कीर्तिश्च मणिना सह ।
प्रादुर्भूतोऽस्मि राष्ट्रेऽस्मिन् कीर्तिमृद्धिं ददातु मे ॥

upaitu māṃ devasakhaḥ kīrtiśca maṇinā saha ।
prādurbhūto'smi rāṣṭre'smin kīrtimṛddhiṃ dadātu me ॥

Mrikanda said, "Please Mother, ages have passed, let go and forgive us now. Such discrimination doesn't befit you. Please distribute yourself equally to all. Anybody should be able to rejoice in you, based on their merit and not on their birth."

That's what Krishna said too, in the Bhagavad Gita. Nobody belongs to a particular caste or *varna*, social class, just because they are born into it. You become what you are, based on your karma. That's how Vishvamitra was able to become a *brahmarshi*.

ब्राह्मणक्षत्रियविशां शूद्राणां च परंतप ।
कर्माणि प्रविभक्तानि स्वभावप्रभवैर्गुणैः ॥

brāhmaṇakṣatriyaviśāṁ śūdrāṇāṁ ca parantapa ।
karmāṇi pravibhaktāni svabhāvaprabhavairguṇaiḥ ॥ BG 18:41 ॥

Mrikanda Rishi thus appeased the Goddess, who said that henceforth she would not discriminate against his clan. Although some remnants of her curse might remain for yugas to come, but mostly it would be alright.

***

Mrikanda Rishi was the father of another magnificent sage called Markandeya Rishi. Markandeya knew that his grandfather had once upset Lord Shiva for no good reason. He also knew that his father had appeased the Goddess. Think of DNA—no matter what we do, it carries traits from generation to generation. So too might the the deities' censure of Bhrigu carry on through time. Markandeya decided to propitiate Lord Shiva because it takes a full lifetime to invoke one energy. He knew that his father, Rishi Mrikanda, couldn't do that task, so he decided to take it on instead. It helped that Markandeya was an ardent devotee of Lord Shiva.

There was a further story behind Markandeya's dedication to the Mahayogi. It so happened that while his father, Mrikanda, looked into his future through Bhrighu Samhita and his penance, he realized that he would have no offspring, no one to carry his knowledge forward. So Mrikanda had prayed intensely to Lord Shiva who told him, "Look, I can't give you a child because it isn't in your fate."

"Since when have you started following the rules, Shiva? You can do anything. You can break any protocol. Please help me here," Mrikanda pleaded. "We desperately need an offspring, because I have all these *vidyas*, knowledge that I need to pass on. And there is an inherent benefit if the receiver of the *vidya* is my own child, because we would have similar characteristics."

Lord Shiva said to him, "Well, I will give you two options then. One, a son who will live long, but will be a dunce, thick-skinned, thickheaded, although very handsome. Two, I will give you a brilliant genius of a son, who will live only until he is 16. Whom would you want?"

Mrikanda rishi replied that it was a no brainer. He looked at his wife and she agreed, absolutely the second one. So they went for the second boon, the result of which was the birth of Markandeya Rishi.

"My grandfather upset Lord Shiva, but then Shiva was the one with whose boon I came to be born, I should really devote my life to him," Markandeya decided one day. His father, Mrikanda, was quite shrewd. After some rumination, he said to Markandeya, "Listen carefully, my son, you are destined to live only till you are 16. If there is any way out, it is only through Shiva. He is the lord of death. Only he can control Yama. If you want to live longer, my recommendation to you would be to seek him." So Markandeya made it an absolute and integral part of his existence to pray daily to Shiva. He spent all his time in a Shiva temple doing Rudram and other chants, along with learning the Vedas.

When the fated moment of his early death arrived, Yama and his messengers came to put a noose around Markandeya's neck. But Markandeya held tightly onto the Shiva lingam, just as a little child would hold on to his mother's leg, and refused to let go. The noose that was thrown for Markandeya encircled the Shiva lingam too.

Lord Shiva manifested right there and said, "What's going on in here? How dare you put a noose around the Shiva lingam, around me?"

Yama said, "Lord, I am just following your protocol!"

"I don't know any protocol, but this is just not right," Shiva said. "You cannot capture him. And you put a noose around me!"

"O Shiva, I am sorry, but You have given me a specific job. I have to do that job, and I am going to do it! Otherwise it would be an extraordinary and unnecessary interference in the workings of nature."

"Did you not hear what I said? Begone!"

"I can't," Yama insisted.

"Are you asking for death?" Shiva said. "Here's my trident, where should it strike your body?"

"I am happy to die, my Lord," Yama replied, "but I have to honor my dharma."

A battle ensued between the two; Yama eventually gave up and conceded defeat. He said, "Lord, at least now, nobody can tell me that I didn't do my part; I tried my best almost till the point of death itself."

Lord Shiva pronounced, "Markandeya will be immortal—he can never be captured by death. He will be one of the eight immortal sages known to mankind."

When Markandeya gained that boon, he continued to pray to Lord Shiva but he also realized the importance of Devi, Mother Goddess. *I must pray to and invoke Mother Divine to complete my sadhana. I must understand the feminine aspect of my penance.*" And so he performed a very rigorous *tapasya* of Mother Goddess in the form of Durga. Eventually, he wrote the Markandeya Purana, from which we get the Durga Saptashati, the quintessential text of Devi worship.

Just like Srimad Bhagavad Gita came out of Mahabharata and Lalita Sahasranama came out of Brahmanda Purana, Durga Saptashati came out of Markandeya Purana.

It is incredible when one person, one soul is awakened, what an extraordinary difference they can make to the world, and to other people's lives. And that is pretty much the basis, the purpose and the result of sadhana. You go on to magnify your existence to such a degree and magnitude that you really elevate yourself and along with that, everybody who looks up to you.

That's why this verse belongs to Mrikanda rishi because he was the first sage to invoke it, to convert it into a mantra. Here, Brahma, Vishnu, and Shiva also represent the three states of consciousness, namely, dreaming, sleeping, and awake. The holy trinity also refers to the three modes of material existence which are *sattva*, goodness, *rajas*, passion, and *tamas*, ignorance. In the present context, they also signify the body, mind and soul. The holy trinity of Brahma, Vishnu, and Shiva also represent the three aspects of time: past, present, and future.

One who has done penance like Bhrigu, naturally gains unimpeded access to the three aspects of everything. Ultimately, one of the things Sage Bhrigu proved is that you need a pure mind, represented by Vishnu, to protect your life. Lord Vishnu is the protector, *bhakta-vatsala*. To operate well in this world, your mind needs to be in the right place. That means you can't live in the past or the future, you have to live here in the present.

क्षुत्पिपासामलां ज्येष्ठामलक्ष्मीं नाशयाम्यहम् ।
अभूतिमसमृद्धिं च सर्वां निर्णुद मे गृहात् ॥८॥

kṣutpipāsāmalāṃ jyeṣṭhāmalakṣmīṃ nāśayāmyaham ॥
abhūtimasamṛddhiṃ ca sarvāṃ nirṇuda me gṛhāt ॥ 8 ॥

(The scripture of Lakshmi Tantra, wherein Mother Goddess expounds on her own names and the various mantras contained in Sri Suktam, omits direct exposition of this mantra by the Divine Mother. This is most probably because it contains no inherent boons or positive mantras.)

Lakshmi and Saturn Trap Narada

Verse 8

Out of the sixteen verses of Sri Suktam, there are two verses from which no mantras have emerged. One such verse is the eighth and the other is the sixteenth. The sixteenth verse is what we call *phalashruti*, the outcome. Think of that as a reward or a promise of a reward.

If your parents have made you a promise, e.g., that if you study they will buy you a new phone, then you are always reminding them of their promise. A *phalashruti* is basically just that. It's a reminder that this is the word of the Vedas; the word of the sages that you will be given a certain reward if you do what they ask you to do.

It is, therefore, perfectly understandable that there are no mantras for sadhana from the sixteenth verse. It is simply the promise of an outcome, after all. But what is particularly interesting, however, is that the eighth verse is not a *phalashruti* and yet, no independent mantras are found in this verse.

No wonder that this verse was first brought to life by the legendary itinerant sage, Narada. For, firmly established in devotion of Lord Vishnu, he has no desires. This verse does not really ask Mother Goddess for anything, directly—it does not request the Goddess to appear, nor does it ask for specific gifts. Instead, it simply appeals that things such as hunger, thirst, want for power and wretchedness be taken out of life. It just seeks that things that bother us be removed.

A reference is made in this verse to Alakshmi, that which is not Lakshmi, that which is undesirable. She's considered the elder sister of Lakshmi. The esoteric idea behind it is that, to get what we desire, one has to go through plenty of grind and undesirable struggle. To get to effortlessness, one has to go through a lot of effort. Simply put, to get to Lakshmi, you have to go through Alakshmi.

Narada chose this verse because he has never prayed to anyone other than Lord Vishnu. So when the time came, he was the right person to invoke this mantra of Sri Suktam. For Narada had nothing to ask for.

In fact, he was cursed by his father, Brahma, and his own brother, Daksha Prajapati. He is a *manasaputra,* created from the mind of Brahma, who wanted him to lead the life of a householder. But Narada had other ideas. Upon repeated entreaties from his father, one day Narada made clear his intent in no uncertain terms.

"I don't want to be a householder, Father," Narada said. "I want to chant the holy name and just go about my life saying, 'Narayana, Narayana'. There is nothing else that I seek, there is nothing else that I want, and nothing else that fascinates me or moves me in any shape or form. This is my final decision and nothing will ever change that."

"What a ridiculous son you are!" Brahma said, rife with agitation. "So be it, then. You will never have a family, and you will just go about the Universe playing your veena, like a nobody. There will never be any offering made to you in any *yajna* nor any portion that comes from the Devas."

Now, Daksha Prajapati is also Brahma's son, and always gets the first offering in any *yajna*. We make that by saying, "*Om Prajapatye Swaha.*"

But Narada was not someone who would apologize to his father and change his mind. Instead, he said, "This egregious behavior is totally uncalled for. You started hurling abuses and cursing me, so I shall also curse you too—you shall never be offered any oblations in any *yajna* either. People will build temples for Vishnu and Shiva but there will be none for you, even though you are the creator. People will not want to have anything to do with you."

So, because of what transpired there is no puja, no temple for Brahma except at Pushkar.

And Narada went on his way saying, "Narayana, Narayana, Narayana..."

When his brother, Daksha's sons were to get married, Narada counseled his nephews that the life of a householder was not all that easy. While it had great fulfillment and pleasures, one would always be on their toes. Narada stressed that marriage was all about constant transactions. You have to continually and tirelessly work for your family. His nephews seemed to nod in agreement.

Seeing their open minds, Narada continued, "You won't be able to roam around much once you are married. The duties of the house will tie you down completely. Why don't you explore the world a little first and see what you really want from your life? I recommend you go around the Universe and just take a look. Do you know how vast it is?"

They shook their heads in unison.

"You haven't even seen the Universe yet and you want to get tied down as a householder and bring up kids?" Narada chastised them. "At least go around the Universe and see how big and beautiful it is. If you feel you are ready for marriage at the end of your expedition, you can always do so."

And so, Narada sent them on a journey from which they would never return, because there is no end to the Universe. The poor innocent souls went on the journey thinking that they would get married on their return. But they never came back, because there are always more and more places in the infinite Universe to go and lose yourself in.

When Daksha found out, he said, "Narada, what kind of a brother are you! My sons would have married and extended the human race, but you sent them on a voyage from which they can never return. I condemn you! You too will live the life of an eternal itinerant."

"So long as I can chant Narayana's name, nothing else matters to me." Narada said.

Narada then used this curse as a blessing in disguise, to spread Vedic dharma. He was the one who, eons ago, first consolidated the various ideologies that existed at the time such as: the Yaksha Sanskriti, belonging to Ravana and Kuber, the Raksha Sanskriti, the culture of Ravana and his clan, the Aryan Sanskriti of the *manavas,* the human race, and the Deva

Sanskriti, the practices of the entities whom we now refer to as gods in the Vedas.

So, Narada never prayed to anybody. If you look at any of the eighteen major Puranas, there is not really much about him praying to Mother Goddess for anything at all, because in his mind he says, "*I am content. I don't have any questions. I don't have any aims and objectives. There is nothing that I seek. Narayana is enough for me.*"

Once it so happened that Shani, the planet Saturn, and Ma Lakshmi met and somehow the topic came about: who among the two was greater?

"I don't think this is even a question," Saturn said. "It's but a foregone conclusion that I am the superior one here!"

"And, how exactly have you arrived at such a fallacious view?" Ma Lakshmi said.

"Well, I create Raja yoga for people," Saturn said haughtily. "I can have somebody sit on a throne or I can toss them to the ground and make a beggar out of them. And all within moments."

"Well yes, but what will they do being a king if I choose not to be there? After all, I am the goddess of wealth and opulence."

"Believe me, when I become favorable and summon the forces of the Universe to create Raja yoga," Saturn said, "even you come running too."

Ma Lakshmi realized that there was no point arguing with Saturn because in any argument when someone starts making baseless claims, it stops being reasonable or meaningful.

Therefore, they agreed that the best way to settle the question would be to seek another person's opinion—someone who would not be biased.

And so they went to the creator, Brahma, and asked him. "Maharaj, we have a question. Please, settle it for us—who amongst the two of us is greater?"

Brahma replied, "I am not getting into that. It's a no-win situation."

He thought that if he displeased Saturn, it wouldn't be good for him. And if he angered Mother Goddess, that would do him no good, either. So he said, "I am an old man and past all these things. I don't know much, so why don't you go to Vishnu? He has an answer to everything, so check with him."

Ma Lakshmi thought if she were to go to Lord Vishnu it would get a bit tricky—how would he disagree with her when she was his consort? But she realized this might actually work out in her favor because the Lord would have to side with her. So they went to Vishnu and asked him who he thought was greater. On one hand Vishnu saw Saturn, who was his nephew. This was because Saturn was the son of Lord Surya, the Sun; and Surya was a cousin of Vishnu from the same clan—the Devas. On the other hand was his own consort. Vishnu thought, *I must not annoy either of them. One is like my son and the other is my better half.*

"Look, right now I am very tired, I need to rest," Vishnu said. "You should go to Lord Shiva instead. He will go deep into samadhi, dhyana, and tell you who is greater."

Shani and Lakshmi decided that since they had already come thus far and taken so much effort, they might as well go all the way, and question Shiva as well.

"Who amongst us is greater?" Shani and Lakshmi asked Bholenath.

Lord Shiva saw the dichotomy, the dilemma of the whole situation, and said, "I just sit here all day, you know. I haven't been around the world, but there is one person who has—Narada. He has seen everybody. He just doesn't stop roaming around. I think he's the best person to answer this question. So, if you don't mind, I will get back to my meditation and you can approach him. In fact, he is just around the corner."

Mother Goddess and Saturn approached Narada and said, "Devarishi, we have a question for you, and you cannot now forward the file to somebody else. You have to resolve it. You have to answer because we have now been to the holy trinity and you are the only one left—so you have to answer this for us!"

Narada said, "What is it?"

"Who of us is greater?" they queried, without beating about the bush.

"Ah, I see, the age old question," Narada smiled. "Just the players have changed. Well, to tell you the truth, both of you are equally great."

"You can't wiggle out of this one, Devarishi," Saturn and Ma Lakshmi spoke in one voice. "Just tell us, who is greater?"

Narada looked at Saturn and then turned towards Mother Goddess.

"It is a very tricky question," he said. "Some questions don't have an answer."

"We don't want to hear any philosophical ruminations. We just need an answer. Resolve this for us and we won't hold it against you."

"Alright then, why don't both of you walk to that tree and then return to me. I would like to observe your gait." Both of them obliged, and when they returned, Narada still gave the same answer and said, "I still think both of you are great; equal to each other."

"Narada," they thundered, "We will curse you if you repeat this one more time! Give us a better answer."

"Alright, alright," he said. "Please walk again for me."

"It's totally clear now," Narada said, after observing them walk one more time. "Saturn, you look good when you are walking away and O Lakshmi, you look the best when you are coming towards me."

"Narayana…Narayana…," he continued, "And now, I am out of here!"

The one thing to learn from Narada's life is his dedication to his cause—spreading the glories of Vedic dharma and of Narayana, and never ever seeking anything from anyone, or from anywhere else at all. Now, when you have that kind of a single-minded focus, when your dedication is superior to that degree, when your devotion is so singular in nature, there may be ups and downs in your life, in fact, there will be, but you will weather every storm. Nothing will be able to crush you, or shake you, or displace you, because you are firmly anchored. That is why in sadhana or elsewhere in life, it is important to just stay focused and have your devotion solely channelized on the one entity you wish to be like. Two is dilution, three—forget it all together, there's no hope. So, you can pray in different forms, but bear in mind that they are all one, it's all the same.

If you do sadhana thinking that since this God or this guru or this person hasn't solved my problems, I will go elsewhere now, you will never be able to solve your problems anywhere at all. If instead you say—let me be patient, let me continue with this, something amazing will come about.

Such is the essence of 'Samudra Manthan', the profound act of churning. It demands the currency of time, supreme effort, unwavering tenacity, and relentless persistence. Without perseverance and focus, sadhana yields few results. And yet, at its core, it is fueled by devotion and hope. Remove any element from this alchemical mix, and the endeavor falters.

All said and done, the sadhana of Sri Suktam does not mean that somehow all great things will become permanent in your life. Nothing is designed to last forever. Yes, wealth can stay, comforts can linger, but not forever. Something we come to understand abundantly in the next, the ninth verse of this remarkable hymn.

गन्धद्वारां दुराधर्षां नित्यपुष्टां करीषिणीम् ।
ईश्वरीं सर्वभूतानां तामिहोपह्वये श्रियम् ॥९॥

gandhadvārāṃ durādharṣāṃ nityapuṣṭāṃ karīṣiṇīm ।
īśvarīṃ sarvabhūtānāṃ tāmihopahvaye śriyam ॥ 9 ॥

I am the ever-existing cause (that produces) all holy fragrances. The brahmins, who are masters in Vedic learning, name me Gandhadvara.

I am invincible against all titans, demons and ogres. Being pure consciousness and pure activity, I cannot be eliminated by any counter-knowledge or act. Since I am consciousness and activity and at the same time the self of all beings, how can a person, desirous of denying me do so by experiencing a negatory knowledge or committing a negatory deed?

No one is capable of going beyond my manifestation as consciousness. As there is no such person, so the scholars of Samkhya knowledge, who regard me as verily being unsurpassable consciousness, call me Duragharsha.

The Legend of Medha Muni

Verse 9

This beautiful verse of Sri Suktam is almost universally used to make a devotional offering of incense or any kind of fragrance in most Vedic rituals. The sage who invoked this is known as Medha Muni, and in various scriptures, he's also referred to as Medhas or Sumedha. Medha Muni is not as renowned as some of the other sages and seers on the path of mantra sadhana, but that does not mean that his contribution is not significant. In fact, this particular verse of the Sri Suktam hymn that was brought to life by Medha Muni is one of the most widely used and potent verses.

It all started when he sought the refuge of Rishi Markandeya. Yes, Markandeya is the same sage I spoke about a couple of chapters ago. After going from pillar to post without the taste of self-realization, Medha ended up at Markandeya's hermitage. To the ordinary eye, Markandeya could be passed off as just any other sage, any seeker for that matter, but Medha sensed that something was extraordinary about this sage. He had no idea that this iconic seer had been granted immortality by none other than Shiva himself.

"I see what brings you here, Medha Muni," Markandeya said in their first meeting. "I also see why you have not realized the truth yet."

"Enlighten me, O Sage," Medha entreated. "I seek your counsel and blessings."

"You are impatient," Markandeya said. "And you are only thinking about yourself, continually. Stay here, be still. Meditate on the Divine Mother while reflecting on the ephemeral nature of this world. Just as fragrance never stays in one place, just as it constantly disperses, so is nothing permanent in this world. Whatever you have today is transient. It belonged to someone else at one time, in the same or different form, and in the future it will belong, yet again, to someone else."

Following this instruction, Medha Muni sat in unflinching penance, and upon realization, chose to stay there and serve Markandeya. He played an important role for which he gets a mention in the scripture Markandeya wrote. Of particular significance is his part in the following story:

Once, there was a king who lost a battle, after which he came back to his kingdom. Even though his army had been much bigger, much greater, and much mightier than that of the enemy king, he had still lost. He came back to his kingdom thinking that he would gather himself and go to battle once again to win back his territory. But it so happened his ministers conspired against him. He then realized that there was no point to it all and quietly, one day, he left his kingdom, much like the Buddha. He realized the selfishness present in the world—in his world at least, and began to question the meaning of all action he had taken thus far. What battle was he fighting? For whom was he fighting? For those people who didn't even belong to him? This king sought refuge in the ashram of Sage Markandeya.

There, he met a merchant who was at that time looking rather miserable and depressed. The king said to the merchant, "You look forlorn, my friend. What's wrong?"

"All my life I have worked very hard," the merchant said. "I had only one habit which my family thought was my weakness; it was that I used to spend a lot of time and money on charity. I have a wife and an only son, and both of them strongly disapproved of my charitable works. They thought that I just wanted to squander away all our money by distributing it at various places, and giving to the needy. They thought that this was not how things were supposed to be done. So one day, they kicked me out of the house. Therefore, in search of the divine, in search of answers, I ended up in this ashram."

He asked the king in return—what had brought him to the ashram? In response, the king told him his story. Both men agreed that there was no point to this world. What is the ultimate truth? Where is liberation, what should we be striving for, and how do we get it?

They approached Markandeya with their questions. The trouble is, though, when you go to someone who's way more advanced than you, there's almost always a huge gap—the gap of understanding and comprehension. A beginner approaches a master looking for concrete steps; but a true master never employs a cookie-cutter, one-size-fits-all approach. In the beginning, you need a teacher. And after you've walked the path a bit, a master can help you. Markandeya knew that without walking the path of self-purification, without penance and deep reflection, they would not be ready to receive direct guidance from him. Not yet, anyway. And so he directed them to Medha rishi.

"Sit down," Medha prompted them. "I see that you are grief-stricken right now. I also see that the seeds of devotion are not even planted in your consciousness, forget about them sprouting."

"How can we cultivate this devotion you speak about, O Muni?" they asked.

"It's hard to be devoted when you don't understand the scale, grandeur and glory of the object of your devotion," Medha Muni replied.

He asked them to pay attention to the glories of Mother Goddess, which he narrated to them both. These were the stories he had heard from Markandeya. Whatever Medha told them, along with the back stories of the merchant and the king, got documented in Markandeya Purana, one of the oldest of the eighteen principal puranas. This subtext in the purana came to be known as Devi Mahatmya, the glories of the Goddess. Comprising of 700 verses, it is also known popularly as Durga Saptashati.

The king's name was Suratha and the merchant's name was Samadhi. Upon hearing the magnificent glories of Mother Goddess, Suratha and Samadhi were moved to tears. They clasped Medha Muni's feet and asked for instructions and blessings so they could also invoke the Divine Mother.

Medha Muni said, "Look, here is a river flowing by. Stay here and do the Durga Saptashati daily. But more importantly, chant the Navarna mantra."

So he initiated them into the Navarna mantra, one of the most awakened and famous mantras of Ma Durga. The mantra of '*aing hreeng kleeng chamundaye vicche*'. Suratha and Samadhi chanted the Navarna mantra with extreme devotion for three years, after which they had a vision of the Goddess. Ma is *mukti-bhukti pradayini*—not only does she grant liberation, she also says that she is *īswarīm sarva bhutanām*—that her opulence is unlimited and she grants her opulence to her devotees.

Now, the king and the merchant had the option of going back to live in the world or to keep doing what they were doing; they both chose different things. For details, I recommend that you read the Durga Saptashati.

Seeing Medha Muni's extraordinary brilliance as well as unparalleled devotion, Markandeya knew that the time had come for the next verse in Sri Suktam to be invoked. The right sage had come along, who was capable of bringing to life one of the verses of the hymn. Both Markandeya and Medha had been ardent worshippers of the nine-lettered mantra. It should, therefore, come as no surprise to anyone that Medha Muni chose the *ninth* verse—after his practice of the Navarna mantra. Not only that, the ninth verse has nine words (tāmih-opahvay are two words):

गन्धद्वारां दुराधर्षां नित्यपुष्टां करीषिणीम् ।
ईश्वरीं सर्वभूतानां तामिहोपह्वये श्रियम् ॥

gandhadvārāṃ durādharṣāṃ nityapuṣṭāṃ karīṣiṇīm ।
iśvarīṃ sarvabhūtānāṃ tāmihopahvaye śriyam ॥

Usually, I refrain from saying such things because most people are eager to use a shortcut, but if you are genuinely pressed for time, know this: the Navarna mantra carries the same potency of Adya Shakti, of the primal energy of Mother Goddess, as does this verse.

Now you know why Medha Muni chose this particular verse and what devotion can do to a seeker. I say that love is the only way to transform an individual. You can strike fear in somebody's heart and extract a certain behavior from them, but that is likely to be temporary. In the end you have to flush their heart, mind, and consciousness with so much love that they would want to change for you and would want to adopt the new way voluntarily.

Similarly, on the path of awakening, devotion is the only way, because devotion alone will soften you. With purely bookish knowledge, the hardened tendencies, our ego, don't really leave us. They may go away for a little while only to come back with a vengeance. Devotion is the only way to smoothen the rough edges, it is the only thing that's going to melt you, that's really going to make you feel that it doesn't matter, nothing matters, nothing matters eventually. The only thing that is eternal in my life is my Divine and me, *Bhagavan* and *bhakta*. Everything has its place, but everything is also secondary—because they will come and go, things will ebb and flow. It's subject to emotions, the cycles of nature, the vicissitudes of time, and the vagaries of human life.

Sometimes this realization happens after you have gained the precious diamond of devotion. Sometimes it happens when you realize the futility of recklessly pursuing the cyclical nature of life—you come to the conclusion that you wish to belong to something that is eternal. That you want to devote life to something that's beyond change.

Kalatita, gunatita, vishvatita—these words refer to being beyond the modes of material nature, beyond this universe, basically referring to the Source. When devotion comes about, our whole perspective towards life changes. Why, our perspective towards everyone around changes. The same thing happened with Medha Muni. He never wrote a Purana of his own but Markandeya rishi lauded him, "You've accomplished an amazing task by narrating the glories of the Devi. So I am going to include you in my purana." Indeed, there is a huge section devoted to him in this purana.

मनसः काममाकूतिं वाचः सत्यमशीमहि ।
पशूनां रूपमन्नस्य मयि श्रीः श्रयतां यशः ॥१०॥

manasaḥ kāmamākūtiṃ vācaḥ satyamaśīmahi ।
paśūnāṃ rūpamannasya mayi śrīḥ śrayatāṃ yaśaḥ ॥ 10 ॥

All desires for objects belonging to the earth, atmosphere or heaven, as well as for the non-material Absolute, which always hold pleasure are contained in me. I am the ultimate basis, upon which all objects of longing are displayed. I surpass everything and am the object of Vishnu's mental longing. Therefore gods praise me as the manasah kama.

That which is known as speech belonging both to the secular and to the sacred, viz. Vedic and external Agamas, whether unpronounced or pronounced, when produced through effort, always refers to me alone. Therefore the scholars of the Vedas infer that I am that which is referred to akuti in all forms of speech whose utterance involves physical effort.

The whole creation, which true knowledge reveals as separated into the two categories of true and false, is myself. Hence the sages call me Satya.

Yakshinis Humble Veda Vyasa

Verse 10

The peerless sage Parashara was passing through the woods when he stopped at the banks of the wide Yamuna river. With the intention of crossing the river, he saw and waved down a boatman. Although the boatman was busy eating his food, he realized that this was a *tapasvin* and it was not good to keep him waiting. So he said to his daughter Matsyagandhi, the one who smelled like fish, "Why don't you take the sage across the river?"

She was a young virgin girl, barely past her puberty, and a little shy too. Her father doted on her with his life. Even the constant smell of fish from her body had felt like the world's finest fragrance to him and so out of love, he had named her *matsyagandhi*. "Sure, Father," she said in response.

The rishi sat in the boat and as they started crossing the river, Parashara looked up at the skies. And he realized that this particular moment was one that came once in a million years. It was a momentous time that would give the world an extraordinary sage.

So, he said to Matsyagandhi, "Will you bear my child?"

"Is this some kind of a joke?" she said, a little hesitantly, but with the petulance of a teenager.

Parashara reiterated his proposition, affirming its seriousness. After some deliberation, Matsyagandhi asked for two boons in return. First, that she would live like a queen so she could have all the resources required to bring up her child; and second, she wanted to permanently get rid of the constant smell of fish from her body.

"Granted," he said with conviction.

"I knew from the moment you came aboard that you are a most revered *tapasvin*, Parashara," Matsyagandhi said. "You are bringing our tribal practices under the recognition of the Vedas too."

It was true that Parashara was not only a scholar and an adept, but deeply admired by royalty and other sages too. He had been positioning that the practices of tantra that were ordinarily looked down upon, but extensively practiced by the tribes and other cultures, be brought under the ambit of the Vedas. This was a big ask—almost like rewriting the constitution, as opposed to just passing a new bill in the parliament. Parashara wasn't expecting a boatman's daughter to know so much. But then again, he was not expecting to be courting a young girl either.

He asked Matsyagandhi to anchor the boat next to a tiny island in the vast Yamuna. A shroud of clouds descended, making the thick fog thicker, and right there, Parashara fathered a son of Matsyagandhi—whose name was later changed to Satyavati. The son she birthed was called Krishna Dvaipayan. Krishna means somebody who is dark, *shyaam varna*, and Dvaipayan means that his residence, his *ayana* was on a *dvipa*, an island. That is, he was born on an island. Krishna Dvaipayan was not an ordinary kid, because he was born under special circumstances by the divine glance and understanding of a sage who was an awakened being himself, and who was unchained by worldly ways.

When Krishna Dvaipayan grew old enough to speak, he asked Matsyagandhi who his father was. She tried to dodge the question a few times. "Tell me, who is my father? Mother, there is this fire raging in me," he confronted her one day. "I do not belong here."

"I don't know what you are talking about," she replied, trying to sound calm.

"Nothing can deter me today," Krishna Dvaipayan said. "I know all about the boons you got when I was conceived."

"Then you must know who your father was, as well," she replied, startled.

"Of course I do," he said, with eyes that held no emotion. "Just bless me then and let me go."

Seeing that there was no way out, she revealed to Krishna Dvaipayan that his father was none other than Parashara himself. She also apprised him that nobody, including Krishna's grandfather, knew about it. Everyone believed that Matsyagandhi had conceived from niyoga, the non-union union, through the power of pure mantras.

Krishna Dvaipayan who was barely seven years old at that time said, "I must go to my father."

"But, you are my only son," she cried. "I need you."

In response, he reminded her that her desire to be the queen of some kingdom was about to bear fruit, and that she would not really need him. Finally, she let him go on the condition that in case she ever needed him in any emergency or otherwise, he would show up and do whatever she would ask of him. She also assured him that she would only exercise such an option if there was absolutely no other alternative left. He gave her his word, and left.

He headed immediately for his father's abode. He tracked him down in the woods and when he finally reached, he fell flat at his father's feet. He did the *dandavat pranam* and said, "I am sure I don't need to introduce myself, I just seek your blessings. You have to guide me."

"What took you seven years to come here?" Parashara said. "I've been waiting for you for seven years. My time to leave this planet is coming soon, but there is still more than a decade left, so I am asking you to devote yourself to sadhana. You will wield great influence in this world because of the sheer power of your knowledge, but you still need to do *tapasya*. You need to do intense *tapas*, sadhana, so you may ascend to the highest level of consciousness."

Parashara held the hand of Krishna Dvaipayan and drew him a bit closer. "My son," he said, "the culture of Bharatvarsha is under threat. Things are getting disunited; so, I need to consolidate the Vedas. I have compiled mantras of the Atharva Veda, which is yet not a recognized Veda, so I need you to go to Hastinapur, the capital of India and start building your network there. Get the scholars on your side, consolidate the Vedas and get them accepted so that ordinary people, normal people, can start chanting."

Samaveda is the book of songs. Rig Veda is the book of *stutis*, hymns and odes. Sri Suktam is from Rig Veda. Yajur Veda is a book of rituals. Atharva Veda is the book of mantras—all the mantras for normal sadhana are in there. Invoking the mantras of Rig Veda would take extraordinary sages, like the ones we have been talking about, who would do nothing else but spend their entire lifetime invoking, sometimes, just one mantra.

Parashara said, "For that compilation you will be known as Veda Vyasa."

Vyasa means compiler. The name stood for 'someone who has combined and consolidated the Vedas'.

Krishna Dvaipayan said, "Father, how can I do that? I am just seven years old, I don't know anybody."

"I am not asking you to go right now," said Parashara. "I want you to do your sadhana and in due course, you will know. Things will happen automatically—your fate, your destiny, your mission, your purpose will take you where you need to be, to fulfill it."

Krishna Dvaipayan retreated into the Himalayan woods and started his sadhana, his *tapas*. As declared by Parashara, Krishna Dvaipayan came to be known as Veda Vyasa. The kind of sage who had no equal, not in the present, past or future. Till date, even five thousand years later, he remains the most significant seer of Sanatana dharma.

In fact, Krishna says in Srimad Bhagavad Gita:

वृष्णीनां वासुदेवोऽस्मि पाण्डवानां धनञ्जय: ।
मुनीनामप्यहं व्यास: कवीनामुशना कवि: ॥

vriṣṇīnāṁ vāsudevo 'smi pāṇḍavānāṁ dhanañjayaḥ
munīnām apyahaṁ vyāsaḥ kavīnām uśanā kaviḥ ॥ *BG 10.37* ॥

Of the greatest sages, I am Veda Vyasa himself. Veda Vyasa was, per our scriptures, one of the *avataras* of Lord Vishnu. He knew he had come to this planet with a specific purpose and nothing could deter him from his mission.

Several years passed as Veda Vyasa spent time in self-reflection, penance, and solitude. In due course, a son, Shukadeva, was born to him. In Skanda Purana, Devi Bhagavatam, Shrimad Bhagavatam and Mahabharata, there are four different versions about the birth of Shukadeva.

Not surprisingly, Shukadeva was an awakened being himself, an enlightened one. He had heard the stories of Bhagavan while still in the womb. So even though there are four different versions of how he was born, all of them agree that he was a liberated soul, right from his birth.

Before Shukadeva was born, it is said that he stayed in the womb much longer than an ordinary child, refusing to come out, saying, "What's there in the outside world? Only suffering, attachment and affliction. I do not wish to come out into this world!"

But at his father's bidding he did come out and after some time passed, Shukadeva declared one day to his father, Veda Vyasa, that he was going away.

"Going where?" Vyasa asked. "To get the firewood?"

"No father, you are omniscient, you should know. I am going, it's time for me to go. All I want to do is to travel around and spread the glories of Bhagavan."

When Vyasa tried to stop his son, Shuka reminded him that sometime ago, Vyasa had done exactly the same thing. That he had left his mother. Despite not getting permission, Shukadeva walked out of the hermitage with Vyasa following him.

"Shuka... Shuka... Shuka... my son, where are you going? I have sadhanas to give you, I have wisdom to impart, you have to join my mission. We have much work to do."

Shukadeva said, "Not for me, father." And he kept going.

At a distance from the hermitage, there was a pond. Sporting in that pond were some damsels, celestial beings, Yakshinis and Apsaras—frolicking around, totally bare, skinny-dipping. Shukadeva was extremely handsome and young. When he passed the damsels, they looked at him and they stayed where they were. Just a few steps behind was Veda Vyasa. As soon as he came closer, they all leapt to their clothes and covered themselves.

Veda Vyasa took a few steps forward and came back. "Very strange," he said to the damsels. "I'm an old sage, and an awakened one. I'm the Veda Vyasa. Shuka, on the other hand, is young. He is yet to learn any sadhana, any *tapas*, anything at all. He doesn't even know the Vedas properly yet. He has only heard the entire Bhagavatam when he was in his mother's womb and he is completely influenced by that one scripture alone. He has chosen his own mission, but I am the liberated one here. I am the son of Sage Parashara, who is one of the *saptarishis*, the grandson of Vasishtha, who in turn was the son of Brahma. How come you covered yourselves? Do you think I am going to pounce on you or leer at you lustfully?"

And the chief of the Apsaras replied, "O Sage, we don't mean any disrespect to you, but there is a fundamental difference between you and Shukadeva."

"Enlighten me!" he said.

"When Shukadeva passed by, gender meant nothing to him, he only saw Vishnu. But you, O wise one, you see the difference. In Shukadeva you saw your son, whereas in us you saw our nakedness. That's why you confronted us to begin with. And just so you know, your son is gone and won't return."

Vyasa was deeply moved by these words. And actually, it can happen to anybody. Sometimes just one sentence not only gives you a new perspective, but changes your life forever. Who knows what that one sentence may be, and from whom it may come? Vyasa made peace with the fact that Shukadeva was not coming back, and he immediately went to Sage Parashara.

"Father," Vyasa said to the aged seer. "I am torn. I did sadhana the way you asked me to, I devoted a lot of time to intense self-reflection. I have made my notes for the compilation of the Vedas and it's going to happen soon, with your grace. But I have just one question. How come I was so deeply attached to my son? Where did all that wisdom, that liberation, that sadhana go? Why was I running behind him like a mad man? Who was he after all? What was he? He will be dead one day, as I will be dead one day. These bodies will perish, so why that attachment? Why do I still have the remnants of those *vikaras*, afflictions, in my consciousness?"

"It is so because until now, I have only been preparing you for the main sadhana," said Parashara. "Now it's time that you started your primary sadhana, and for that, here is the Sri Suktam, which came at the time of the great churning of the ocean, blessed by Lord Narayana himself. He is one of the sages who has invoked verses in this, as has Brahma invoked verses, and other sages too. So it's time for you to pick the next verse and bring it to life."

And the tenth verse of the divine hymn was imparted to him.

मनसः काममाकूतिं वाचः सत्यमशीमहि ।
पशूनां रूपमन्नस्य मयि श्रीः श्रयतां यशः ॥

manasaḥ kāmamākūtiṃ vācaḥ satyamaśīmahi ।
paśūnāṃ rūpamannasya mayi śrīḥ śrayatāṃ yaśaḥ ॥

Parashara continued, "Seek Her refuge alone. Your sadhana will not be complete unless you invoke Mahavidya."

Vyasa went back and started to invoke this verse with extraordinary detachment. He found all his heart's desires fulfilled, and also found his happiness, his joy, his devotion and much else, from the sadhana of this verse. But obviously, this was not the full sadhana. This was just the beginning of his main spiritual practice. Parashara Rishi went on to give him another verse of Sri Suktam, and then the full sadhana of Sri Vidya.

"You are everything there is, O Mother! Give me wisdom, give me your grace, so that I seek your refuge alone and nothing else, nowhere else," Vyasa prayed. And such was Vyasa's mind. It is written multiple times, in various scriptures, that when you start to move towards *siddhi*, the attainment of any mantra, one of the things that arises is profound creativity that springs forth along with extraordinary humility. Secondly, profound, genuine, truthful, insights come about. When somebody is humble, when their insight is not their own, they will not pass it on as theirs. We are acknowledging every single sage in these verses.

So, when you move towards *siddhi*, you become very humble. And that's what happened with Vyasa here. As he started to get into the sadhana, he became secluded, he became more of a recluse and he thought to himself, "I don't want to do anything with the world. My father has tasked me with the mission which I have to accomplish, but right now, I don't feel like it." So he went back to the woods to continue his journey. Meanwhile, Sage Parashara, extended his life by some more time, because he realized, "I have put my son on this path and I need to be around longer to see this mission through, or at least get him started on it."

With ten verses already invoked, as the sonic form of Lakshmi inched towards completion, strangely, it was Mother Goddess herself who became alarmed. Somewhere, her concern was genuine too. She knew she had to intervene soon, or she might end up disintegrating into a ruthless world of desires and greed.

कर्दमेन प्रजाभूता मयि सम्भव कर्दम ।
श्रियं वासय मे कुले मातरं पद्ममालिनीम् ॥११॥

kardamena prajābhūtā mayi sambhava kardama ।
śriyam vāsaya me kule mātaraṃ padmamālinīm ॥ 11 ॥

When engaged in creation, I limit the six courses of creation. Being the principle of measurement, I measure everything according to units of measurement. I am the knowledge acquired through all senses and when the time of dissolution comes I embrace all creation within myself.

I carry the whole of creation across the shoreless ocean of created existence; beyond the reach of the ocean of all imperfection, I float in the minds of the living beings. Transformed into clouds I flood the entire creation with rainwater. I am ever concerned about the happiness and welfare of all creatures and act accordingly, therefore the yogins know me as the mother of all creatures.

When Mother Goddess Asked for a Boon

Verse 11

As the verses of Sri Suktam were being brought to life by the sages, in the silent waters of Lakshmi's mind arose a thought that troubled her.

"O Janardana, You are completely detached and in a way, so am I," she said to Lord Vishnu while he was resting. "I course through material existence, weaving the fabric of all trade, commerce and life itself. Yet, I cannot help but confess my disquiet, for it seems you are intent on bestowing me to the world, my essence laid bare for all to behold."

The world was a material place before She even emerged from the ocean. *Kardamenaprajabhuta*—from a very moist ground has She come about. Everything, her *praja*, subjects, *prajanan*, all creation, all flora and fauna has emerged from the moist ground.

"O Narayana," she continued, "if my sonic form is brought to life by everyone else, how would I maintain my constant bond with you? You are Padmanabha, carrying a lotus in your solar plexus, and I am Padmini, seated on a lotus. I beseech you to invoke at least one verse, so I remain intertwined in eternal union with you."

Vishnu showered his benevolent smile on the anxious goddess. He knew that Lakshmi was not unaware of his divine potency. She was fully conscious of the fact that the brilliant Vishnu had a solution for every problem. She was unwilling to accept that anything was beyond reach for Narayana. Besides, she felt his boundless love in every waking moment. And the goddess was completely right on all counts.

"How can I deny what's rightfully yours, Kamale," Vishnu said. "I will take an *avatara*, reincarnate as a sage, and invoke a verse of Sri Suktam."

"When, how, where?" Lakshmi asked, in eager anticipation.

"All in good time. All in the family," he said, and looked into her eyes with much love and reassurance.

***

Kardama sat in searing *tapasya*, penance, with the sole purpose of his existence being his devotion to Lakshmi-Narayana. After invoking three verses with his brother Chiklīta, Kardama was already self-realized. He cared about nothing in the world except for being in eternal meditation of Vishnu, his own father in some ways. And yet, he was not unaware of the fact that at some point in time, he had to make a family, he had to procreate to further the lineage.

One day, while Kardama was deep in meditation, Vishnu appeared before him in his *chaturbhuja*, four-armed form. Kardama felt his entire existence melt away, like butter in fire. The same majestic Vishnu, whom he deeply adored and revered, stood adorned with a vibrant blue hue, representing the boundless expanse of the creation he governed. A magnificent crown rested on the head of Hrishikesha, one of curly hair. Everything on his perfect form was regal, while his four arms held the sacred conch, the discus, the mace, and the lotus, each symbolizing his omnipotence, cosmic order, strength, and purity.

"Ask whatever it is you wish for," Vishnu said, with a gentle smile.

The sage said that he never got to experience bonding with Vishnu as a family. "I was born fully aware of my surroundings, and then upon invoking the second verse, I was sent away to invoke the third and the fourth with Chiklīta. I long to serve you, O Madhusudana. I pine for you how a father misses his son." Kardama replied that all he wanted was more of Vishnu, and in the course of that beautiful conversation, he asked for Vishnu to be born as his son.

Vishnu reminded him that for Kardama to have an offspring, he would have to get married and take a wife. The sage agreed to enter the life of a householder, so Vishnu could be born to him as his son.

A few months later, Swayambhu Manu along with his consort, Shatarupa, and their daughter, Devahuti, paid a visit to the sage. When they entered his hut, he spread a mat on the floor inviting them to sit. Manu and Shatarupa sat, but Devahuti didn't.

She thought, "My parents have brought me here because they would like me to serve this sage and be his other half or better half. So it would not be appropriate for me to sit in front of my would-be husband like that." Sage Kardama saw the humility and the modesty in that gesture. He spoke to her, "Please take a seat."

He decided in that very moment that Devahuti was fit to be the mother of an incarnation of Vishnu. For, the most important trait that's needed to be one with God is humility, and Kardama noticed that she had it in plenty. Manu and his wife presented the marriage proposal.

"It is my good fortune that your goddess-like daughter would be my wife," Kardama said. "But, it is my duty to tell you that my consciousness is yoked to Vishnu, who is my father, godfather, spiritual father, and everything, for that matter. She is going to bear an extraordinary child, but I will never be able to play the role of a traditional husband. Praying to Vishnu and penance are two integral parts of my routine. So if my lifestyle and my intentions are acceptable to Devahuti and you, her parents, I am then willing to solemnize this marriage."

Manu and Shatarupa looked in the direction of Devahuti with a sense of worry, but her shy smile and nod immediately put their concerns to rest. They might not be fully aligned with the views of the sage, but none could deny that having an extraordinary saint immersed in his own world as Devahuti's husband, was better than having an ordinary but lustful man.

The marriage took place and Kardama went back right away to his sadhana. You might think it's a bit unusual that somebody could be so immersed in sadhana that they get married and they're back at their practice. But as you intensify your practice, you realize that this world is nothing but a play. You're simply enacting a certain role and because you are so good at your role-play, it feels like the actor is the character, and the character is the actor. But in reality, what happens is that you are not even here, as you gain more proximity to the divine soul in you.

Sage Kardama went back to his sadhana and a good few years passed. Devahuti kept serving him, and doing the chores, and soon one day, he said to her, "Oh lady, I'm quite pleased with you. What do you want?"

"What do I want!" she exclaimed. "I'm your wife. You promised me that you will give me a son."

"Oh yes, I forgot all about that. I did make you that promise."

And then he reminded her that he had made it clear when the proposal was accepted that after their marriage, he would be back to being a *sanyasi*, and would be on his own path. It was a condition that Devahuti had accepted, thinking that even a bit of time in the presence of the awakened sage would set her free, forever. Now, when Kardama Rishi reminded her of the condition that he set, that he would father a child with her but then, would be back on his own and immersed in his sadhana, she said, "That is fine."

First they had nine daughters—Sati Anasuya who became the consort of Sage Atri, was one of them. Most of the daughters were married—seven of them to the seven great sages, the *saptarishis*. Now naturally, Kardama had to wait to get back to his sadhana, because the son he promised hadn't arrived yet. So, they spent a good few years, two or three decades, raising their daughters. And then, eventually, Lord Vishnu was born as Kapila Muni, the same brilliant saint and scholar who is the key propounder of Sankhya yoga.

Sankhya comes from the Sankrit word meaning 'to count'. Sankhya yoga talks about Purusha and Prakriti; three modes of material nature or *sattva*, *rajas*, and *tamas*; three states of consciousness, and so on.

When Kardama offered the verse of Sri Suktam for invocation to Kapila Muni, who was verily a form of Vishnu, Kapila Muni decided that he wanted sage Kardama to be known as the seer of the mantra. To be sincere to a cause or someone for a short while is something many can do, but to demonstrate lifelong sincerity is rare. And Kardama had done just that. He had been sincere to the path of sadhana throughout his life, without ever worrying about fame, glory, rewards; on the contrary, he shunned them. Kardama was once offered a place among the seven sages, to be one of the *saptarishis*, but he had turned it down. His humility, his sincerity, was not lost on Vishnu. Nothing is lost on Vishnu, for that matter.

It is, therefore, no coincidence that he's the seer of the eleventh verse of Sri Suktam, and that his own name finds a mention in the verse itself. In this verse, the Lord says, "I hereby set the protocol to honor our parents."

कर्दमेन प्रजाभूता मयि सम्भव कर्दम ।
श्रियं वासय मे कुले मातरं पद्ममालिनीम् ॥

kardamena prajābhūtā mayi sambhava kardama ।
śriyaṃ vāsaya me kule mātaraṃ padmamālinīm ॥

This is one of the best verses for a householder. If you might have noticed, I've never really spoken about what a verse brings to you, whether it's wealth, opulence, peace in the family, fulfillment of wishes or whatever else, because I feel that when we do that, then you get distracted as a sadhaka. You focus more on the outcome of the sadhana, than actually focusing on the sadhana itself.

It's much better to do any sadhana just for the grace of it and see what it unfolds for you. The eleventh verse of Sri Suktam is one of the least romantic verses, but it's one of the most potent ones because it was invoked by Lord Vishnu himself. This verse is particularly useful for a householder who wishes to have a peaceful family life.

Kardama rishi gave up his body soon after initiating Kapila Muni into the path of sadhana.

That's one of the fundamental differences between those who are awakened and those who are on the path. When somebody's awakened, they know why they are doing something and they don't cling to it when it's done.

आरुरुक्षोर्मुनेर्योगं कर्म कारणमुच्यते ।
योगारूढस्य तस्यैव शमः कारणमुच्यते ॥

ārurukṣormuneryogaṁ karma kāraṇamucyate ।
yogārūḍhasya tasyaiva śamaḥ kāraṇam ucyate ॥ BG 6.3 ॥

Krishna says, "The one who's fully mounted the path of yoga, Kaunteya, remains unattached to their karma. In fact, it's perfectly fine even if they don't do any karma."

There are no coincidences on the path of sadhana. *Ekadashi*, the eleventh day of the lunar calendar, is the day of Vishnu, and this is the eleventh verse of the hymn. When somebody wants to pray to Lord Vishnu on *ekadashi* then the Sri Suktam is very powerful, because you are acknowledging the presence of feminine energy, the feminine principle, divine energy and the Mother Divine herself. If those who are Srividya *upasakas* or just believe in the form of Devi, or feel an affinity towards it chant this whole Suktam on *ekadashi*, it's even more powerful.

After having brought to life the eleventh verse, where the seer is none other than Bhagavan himself, the next one had to be invoked by someone quite phenomenal again, an extraordinary sage.

आपः सृजन्तु स्निग्धानि चिक्लीत वस मे गृहे ।
नि च देवीं मातरं श्रियं वासय मे कुले ॥१२ ॥

āpaḥ sṛjantu snigdhāni ciklīta vasa me gṛhe ।
ni ca devīṃ mātaraṃ śriyaṃ vāsaya me kule ॥ 12 ॥

(This verse, as in verse eight, has no inherent or new mantras not already covered. Therefore, once again, the Divine Mother does not expound on this verse in Lakshmi Tantra.)

The Penance of Mudgala

Verse 12

In Rig Veda and Srimad Bhagavatam, there is the mention of a dynasty whose people had the prefix 'Aja'. The sage of the twelfth verse of Sri Suktam is Ajas, who belongs to the dynasty of Aja. In Rig Veda, there's a term that refers to them as being good, Ajameda.

When we examine the Vedic tradition from the ancient eras, we get an idea of how our ancestors were. The people in the Ajameda dynasty were so exceptional that they were awarded the title of Aja. For instance, Shankaracharya was a person, but eventually it became a title.

In that dynasty, there was a sage called Mudgala. He got the title of Raja rishi, the royal sage. He was considered at par with Vishvamitra because both were born kshatriya kings, but by the power of their penance, they ascended to the highest realm of consciousness and got the title of a sage. Vishvamitra even got the title of *brahmarshi*.

Mudgala was married to Nalayani, the daughter of King Nala and Damayanti. Like many great kings and sages, he realized very early on, that material pursuits would take him only so far. Mudgala figured that winning more kingdoms would not lead to more happiness, gaining more territories would not necessarily lead to greater fulfillment in life. He was the king of what used to be called the Panchala Kingdom, which is present day Punjab. But at that time, it used to be spread all the way from the Himalayas till the Naimisha forest—east of present day Uttar Pradesh. It was a huge kingdom, a major state.

One of Mudgala's daughters was Ahalya, who eventually got married to the sage Gautama. Mudgala was deeply devoted to Lord Vishnu, and his pious wife, Nalayani, took great interest in listening to the glories of Vishnu from her husband. Gradually, she found herself pining for Vishnu and started imagining how marvelous it would be if she were the consort of Lord Vishnu himself. Mudgala was much older than Nalayani and also in a frail condition. Above all, he was not interested in extending his family, something Nalayani wanted dearly.

"I am sorry to confess this to you," she said to the sage one day, "but I think I am deeply in love with Lord Vishnu."

"What's so surprising about that?" Mudgala replied with the calmness and nonchalance of an awakened sage. "Even I am deeply in love with Lord Vishnu, who wouldn't be?"

Nalayani expressed her desire to have a vision of Vishnu, enquiring why Vishnu couldn't live with them or be a more integral part of their lives, physically. Mudgala, a true devotee, replied that he was not keen on bothering Lord Vishnu, and that he was just happy to be firmly established in Vishnu-consciousness. Nalayani pressed with her desire, saying that in this life Mudgala was her husband but in some lifetime, she would like to be Vishnu's consort. She wondered if there were anything she could do, or any sadhana that would make her desire possible.

"You can't have Vishnu by praying to Vishnu," Mudgala said to Nalayani. "Mother Goddess won't approve of it. So, you have to pray to Shiva and you can do that when I'm gone, which is not too far in the future. I've been asked by Lord Vishnu to invoke this verse of Sri Suktam so that Divine Mother becomes a part of the elements in consciousness, in creation, as well as in people's families. Once that's done, I'll drop this mortal frame."

Mudgala went on to do intense penance, and he ascended to the title of Raja rishi. Thereafter, anyone born in the Ajameda dynasty automatically received the honorary title of Aja. Eventually the Ajas spread throughout India with a predominant concentration in present-day Rajasthan. That's how the city, Ajmer, got its name. Although there are some other stories which say that in the fourteenth century, the king Ajay of Rajasthan built Ajay Sumeru—the Great Cliff, because of which the city got the name Ajmer. Earlier texts, however, credit the Ajas of Ajameda clan. The brilliant Aja people congregated as Brahmins in Karnataka. In that region there's a place called Mudgala where variations of that surname are found—Mudgil, Modgil, and so on. But mostly, the Mudgalas stayed in the Panchal region.

Sage Aja, which in this case is Rishi Mudgala, invoked the beautiful twelfth verse with extreme devotional sentiment for Lord Vishnu. What he had always known, however, was that Lord Vishnu was incomplete without Mother Goddess. For instance, when you organize a family function, you feel more comfortable when you invite other families, and not other bachelors, right? Families like to hang out with families. Bachelors like to hang out with bachelors. Sage Mudgala invited the whole family. He invoked Chiklīta as well, the *manasaputra*, of Vishnu and Lakshmi born at the time of the great churning of the ocean.

Meanwhile, Nalayani did not give up on her dream. She wanted Vishnu and she had her husband's permission. Just before he dropped his body, Mudgala rishi said to her, "Listen, if you really want Vishnu as a spouse, I'm telling you it's not possible. But if there is any chance at all of it happening, only one person in the whole Universe can bring it about. And that person is Lord Shiva. You have to pray to Shiva. How long he will take to come is anybody's guess, but he alone can make it happen. It may take years or decades or lifetimes or eons or kalpas. Nobody can predict it, as that is entirely up to him."

"I will do just that," Nalayani said, with the resolve of a woman in love.

"Fine," Mudgala said, "But remember, I don't think you can have him in the manner you seek. You've been warned."

"That doesn't mean I can't try," Nalayani said, unsurprisingly.

Meanwhile, their daughter, Ahalya, got married to the magnificent scholar sage, Gautama, who composed remarkable treatises on governance and natural laws, known as *nyaya-shastra*. Call it fate or a weak moment, but Ahalya consummated her relationship with Indra. Gautama cursed Ahalya and turned her into a boulder when he found out about her infidelity. It is important to note that Nalayani, her mother, had been married to Mudgala, who was much older than her. And, they married their daughter Ahalya to Gautama, who was also much older in age.

Many countless years passed, and when Lord Vishnu reincarnated as Rama, he touched the boulder with his big toe turning it back into Ahalya. At Rama's instruction, and upon self-realization too, Gautama took back Ahalya.

"This is an unusual bond, Ahalya," Lord Rama said with a smile. "Your father always prayed *to* me. Your mother always prayed *for* me. Your husband is a *mahatapasvin*, a siddha who invoked me and my feminine energy. You are one of the reasons why I had to take this *avatara*—I had to liberate you. And your mother is one of the reasons why I'll have to take the next one, because with her every breath, she has been praying for me. She has been through several lifetimes already, but in every lifetime she picks up from where she left off."

Nalayani continued praying to Lord Shiva and one day, after ages, it yielded the desired result as Shiva manifested his form and asked her what she wanted.

"O omniscient Shiva," she said, "You know what I want. I want Vishnu as my husband."

Shiva told her that it was not possible, that if she so wished she could be immortal, but not Vishnu's consort.

Not one to give up, she said, "There has to be some way. What if I don't know that reality is hidden from me, and that person is exactly like Vishnu. Would that do? In my mind, I would think that he is Lord Vishnu but I wouldn't know the actual truth that he isn't; but he should have all the attributes of Lord Vishnu."

"Are you sure you would be happy with that?" Shiva asked.

"In the absence of a better alternative," Nalayani replied with a sense of dejection in her voice, "I will accept this compromise. That person should have all the attributes of Vishnu."

"Nalayani, it's still not possible," Shiva said, "but I'll tell you what *is* possible since that's the only boon you've asked for. Something similar to what you desire will happen. It is not possible for one person in the world to have all the attributes that Lord Vishnu possesses. He is the ultimate, he is the finest, he is Purushottama—and there can only be one 'finest'. It's a superlative. So, you will have His attributes, but they will be distributed amongst various people. Lord Vishnu is bound to take *avatara* again and when he reincarnates, you will have his presence around you, throughout your life. He will guide you, he will be there for you every step of the way, but you cannot marry him. You cannot be his wife, you cannot have him as your husband. I've done what's best, what's possible, and I'm moving on."

So saying, Lord Shiva disappeared after giving her that boon.

Nalayani was later born as Draupadi and she got five husbands, because it was not possible to have all attributes of Lord Vishnu in just one person—the wisdom, the beauty, the form, the valor, the strength and so on that she wanted was not possible in any one person. But throughout her life she had Krishna, the complete incarnation of Vishnu, by her side, who stood by her through thick and thin, through all her highs and lows.

So that is the story of Sage Ajas, or Ajas Rishi, who invoked this verse and who then blessed anybody who chants this verse.

Naturally, when undertaking the powerful sadhana of Sri Suktam, a question arises: can sadhana fulfill your material goals in life?

If the effort is intact, sadhana can make you a worthy recipient. No question about it. What some of these stories also illustrate is the fact that it can take lifetimes. We cannot make everything happen in our desired timeframe. We cannot say, I want this and only this, or I want this now and I want it in this shape. That's just too many conditions. Nature doesn't care about these. To have that level of autonomy in the Universe, you really have to be operating at a very high level of consciousness. And sadhana is anybody's way of reaching that level of consciousness, and that's what makes the whole path of sadhana worth walking. That's what makes it absolutely beautiful, whether it's extreme self-purification you seek or something beyond.

योगरतो वा भोगरतो वा सङ्गरतो वा सङ्गविहीनः ।
यस्य ब्रह्मणि रमते चित्तं नन्दति नन्दति नन्दत्येव ॥

yogarato vā bhogarato vā saṅgarato vā saṅgavihīnaḥ ।
yasya brahmaṇi ramate cittaṃ nandati nandati nandatyeva ॥
Bhaja Govindam verse 20 ॥

It doesn't matter, Shankaracharya says, *what state of mind you are in, whether you are practising sadhana and self-purification, or enjoying the pleasures of the world. The one who's in constant union with constant remembrance of the Divine, is the one who actually enjoys the most.*

Whenever I chant the Sri Suktam, it never ceases to amaze me, it baffles me, totally. What an incredible hymn this is. Each verse of this hymn has been invoked by a different sage over thousands and thousands, even hundreds of thousands of years. It has taken thousands of years to make a hymn so potent and so powerful. I don't know of any other hymn which is as elaborate in its invocation and as well endorsed from a traditional Vedic point of view,. as the Sri Suktam. Just think about it: to have all these glorious sages, all these amazing seers and the Lord himself. At Divine Mother's behest and asking, and with her own instructions, a hymn has been invoked where each verse is its own mantra and each verse then holds multiple mantras. Just think about it, what a treasure we are sitting on.

And now to put it in perspective, in Sri Vidya, this is only one of the foundational steps. In Sri Vidya you have Sri Suktam, Lalita Sahasranamam, and *panchadasi* mantra; and if you want to have the energy field of Divine Mother, then you use Shri Yantra as well. But without Sri Suktam, you cannot invite her, you cannot invoke her, you cannot make the 16 offerings you would normally do to make her energy really a part of you. It is with Her grace alone that one can pray to Her. Besides, no sadhana ever goes waste. It will yield its own results in its own time. And I think that, in itself, deserves celebration.

आर्द्रां पुष्करिणीं पुष्टिं पिङ्गलां पद्ममालिनीम् ।
चन्द्रां हिरण्मयीं लक्ष्मीं जातवेदो म आवह ॥१३॥

ārdrāṃ puṣkariṇīṃ puṣṭiṃ piṅgalāṃ padmamālinīm ।
candrāṃ hiraṇmayīṃ lakṣmīṃ jātavedo ma āvaha ॥ 13 ॥

I cause all beings to wax in beauty, fame and wealth. I alone lead the pushkara, the lotus-formed entity called time eternal. Hence the sages call me Pushkarini.

Due to my complexion of pure gold I am of a tawny colour. In ancient times I gave Pinga, the king of the Yaksas, great wealth. O Shakra, formerly the king of Yakshas addressed me as Pingala.

O Shakra (Indra), it is myself who am present in all embodied beings as the sushumna duct in their bodies with the view to the final liberation of all souls who are distressed in the samsara. Running from the bottom of the navel to the top of the head ranged over that shakti, there are thirty-two lotuses called the supports, adhara. Since I pervade this row of lotuses, I am envisaged as wearing a garland of lotuses. As I incorporate prakriti, the Person and the time eternal, I am called Padmamalini.

The Tribes of Rudra

Verse 13

The Rudras were the most secluded tribes of the forests. Amongst them, there were 11 heads of states covering the vast and growing empire, and recognition of Shiva. Lord Vishnu also had his own tribe known as the Adityas that had 12 members in the governing council, with Lord Vishnu being the chief. Lord Shiva, on account of his *tapas*, power, heritage and fame, was considered a god, a Deva. But Shiva did not like the fact that the Devas ignored the Yakshas and Rakshasas.

He said, "They existed before us, we, the Devas, have colonized them." And, this was exactly what had happened. The Devas were more intelligent, superior in evolution, technology and application, and they took over in a manner similar to how the Europeans in modern history colonized Australia uprooting the aborigines, or settled in the USA and negated the existence of native Americans.

The Devas were very smart and they said to the Rakshasas, "You will have to pay us tributes to pledge your allegiance to us." And more importantly, because they were quite intelligent, they kept on discovering more and more things such as gemstones, precious stones, gold and other things that would make their kind more dominant.

Lord Shiva, however, strongly disapproved of displacing the older and local cultures, or making them subservient.

"I understand you have to run this creation and you are the undisputed God of the gods," he said to Lord Vishnu once, "but I think we need to be kinder to the Yakshas and Rakshasas. And we need to acknowledge the fact that they exist and they've been here before us. And even though they're slightly different from us, they also deserve all the riches in the world."

"Hey Neelakantha, there is no question about it, O Shankara!" Lord Vishnu replied. "The trouble is that these people are ostentatious, spendthrifts and self-centered. If we empower them any more, they're not going to do anything for the world. They just live for themselves and their ways are quite savage."

"Let's agree to disagree," Shiva said. "Besides," he continued, "I don't want anything to do with the riches, these temples, palaces, Amaravati and the like. I'm happy to just go sit in a cave and be quiet."

"It seems then," Vishnu said with a smile, "I must bear the burden of an opulent life."

Shiva, over a period of time, put together a huge army. These were the *ganas*, the other people in the forests who were outlawed or did not belong to any particular tribe. Shiva said, "I will give you refuge."

Lord Vishnu kept on governing the way he thought was right, to further humanity and Vedic culture. Now, something interesting happened. One of the illustrious sages, Rishi Pulastya—one of Narada's brothers—had a son called Vishrava.

Vishrava was a saint who entered into a tribal marriage similar to what we call an intercaste or interracial marriage. He married twice. First, he married the daughter of Sage Bharadwaj who, although a *Homo sapiens*, had achieved godlike status by virtue of his penance. His daughter was referred to by two different names in different scriptures. One was Ila Vida, the other Ida Vida.

Vishrava later had an intertribal marriage with another girl who belonged to the *H. heidelbergensis* species. Her name was Kaikeshi, and she was the daughter of a powerful Rakshasa king, Sumali.

One day, he drew his beautiful and brilliant daughter, Kaikeshi, closer and said, "You are very beautiful and very intelligent, Kaikeshi, so you must marry somebody who is powerful. If we want to bridge this gap between different species, if we have to further humanity and have our place in it, you will have to marry somebody who wields certain influence across the various tribes and species. Otherwise, we will be erased out of the Vedas. We'll be erased out of history and this will be held against us."

Some battles must be fought not because you care so much about victory but legacy, for one day the "present" will complain that "history" was quiet.

Sumali convinced Sage Vishrava to marry his daughter, positing that she would bear him powerful children who would be wise too. Although Vishrava tried to wriggle out of the arrangement by saying that he was already married to the daughter of a powerful sage, Sumali still persisted, and gave his consent. Kaikeshi, too, readily agreed.

Through Ila Vida—Bharadwaj's daughter, a son Vishravan, also known as Kubera, was born to Sage Vishrava, who was a bridge between the Yakshas, Rakshasas and humans. And, through Sumali's daughter, Kaikeshi, another son called Ravana was born unto him. Although Kubera and Ravana were half-brothers, Ravana was more Rakshasa-like. He was influenced by his maternal grandfather who trained him from a very young age to take over his kingdom one day, and to protect their interests. Kubera, on the other hand, was guided by the Sage Vishrava and Pulastya to do what was good for the world, and to further the cause of humanity as they were going through a period of identity crisis.

Kubera performed intense penance and because of his brilliance and intelligence, he built a vast kingdom. Both Kubera and Ravana were staunch worshipers of Lord Shiva who ruled that entire region. Shiva told them, "I don't need any royalties or tributes from you. You are free to do what you want to. I'm okay with it. Just let me live in peace and don't disturb my people." His people were the *ganas* and also some of the Vānaras who lived freely in the forests. They were never hunted, they were never touched and they were never killed. And that is why it was a big deal when Ravana attacked the Vānara army.

Once Ravana, with his cousins, went to Kubera's kingdom named Lanka and saw that Lanka was a magnificent place. There was so much affluence, it was mostly made of gold and other precious things. People were healthy and rich, and there was abundance in everything.

Sage Pulastya warned his grandson, Kubera, "Look, I am telling you, Ravana is guided by Sumali, his maternal grandfather, and he has an ulterior motive for being here. So now that he's here, he will want to extend his stay. Don't let him."

"Ravana is totally subservient to me," Kubera said, with nonchalance. He was of such opinion because Ravana had approached him with utmost humility and reverence.

Ravana was a brilliant man, a genius, extremely suited for politics and ruling. And he saw that while Kubera was a good person, he was not a good ruler. He was too kind, too gentle. Ravana knew that you couldn't rule a country just by being kind and gentle. You have to make hard decisions. So, gradually it happened over the next many months, that Ravana extended his stay, and eventually totally took over all of Lanka. He built a mutiny within the ranks. And he said to Kubera, "Either I kill you or you leave on your own. What do you want to do?"

Kubera was in complete shock.

"I let you in, Ravana," he said. "I offered you refuge. I thought you were here just for a bit of a vacation."

"I don't know what you thought," Ravana said, "but I'm telling you what I think right now, and that is, Lanka is not good for you. This place belongs to me. This place has always belonged to my ancestors." Kubera asked him what he was talking about as they were the sons of the same father. Ravana reminded him that they belonged to different tribes even though they had the same father. Ravana kicked Kubera out of Lanka.

Talking about tribes, Krishna says in the Bhagavad Gita:

रुद्राणां शङ्करश्चास्मि वित्तेशो यक्षरक्षसाम् ।
वसूनां पावकश्चास्मि मेरुः शिखरिणामहम् ॥

rudrāṇāṃ śaṅkaraścāsmi vitteśo yakṣarakṣasām ।
vasūnāṃ pāvakaścāsmi meruḥ śikhariṇām aham ॥ BG 10.23 ॥

Of the Rudras, I am Lord Shiva himself. Among the Yakshas and Rakshasas, I am Kubera (the treasurer). Of the Vasus, I am fire and I am Meru among the mountains.

What Krishna was trying to tell Arjuna at that time was: don't go after different tribes, different labels, different species. Everything is me. It's the same soul coursing through every living entity.

The Yakshas were the treasurers of the Devas. Ravana saw that if he became the treasurer, like Kubera, he would have great control over the wealth.

Naturally, the question arises, why was Lanka so important? Why did Kubera become the treasurer? Why did the Yakshas become the treasurers of the gods and their wealth? It's important to understand that when the Devas ruled over the entire planet, kings in different parts of the world would regularly send them tribute in the form of money. And that 10% of royalty had to be gathered and collected at a particular place before it could be sent out to the Devas. And in that region, that place was Lanka. So that's why the Yakshas became the treasurers and took a certain fee from the Devas to maintain their treasures. Ravana, however, had other objectives. He claimed that they should get a part of the wealth which was collected, and not just a fee, after all, they were the ones who were gathering this wealth and looking after it. Ravana vastly expanded his empire when he took over Lanka.

Presently, Kubera went to his father Vishrava with his tale of woe. His father told Kubera that he was no match for the mighty Ravana, and that it was best to just set up a new kingdom elsewhere. There was no point fighting against Ravana, because no one could outmaneuver that brilliant man, his father advised.

Unconvinced, Kubera went to his grandfather, Pulastya, and pleaded his case. He knew that being one of the *saptarishis*, his grandfather had the ear of Indra and Vishnu. Pulastya told him that Ravana was a strongheaded person who wouldn't listen to anyone. Since Ravana was very dear to Lord Shiva, Kubera had concluded that there was no point in going to Shiva. He asked Pulastya if he should go to Lord Vishnu instead.

"No point going to Vishnu," Pulastya said. "The solution Vishnu will give you may not appeal to you. He leans a bit more towards the Devas. So I'm not sure if you'll get the best solution. And he's definitely not going to send his army to help you fight Ravana, if that's what you're asking, because Devas don't fight amongst themselves; Lord Vishnu is going to encourage you to do the same. Go to Shiva. He's impartial."

Kubera went to Shiva who laughed, listening to Kubera's plight. He put a bit of firewood in his *dhuni* that was going on at that time, took a puff from his *chillam*, and a swig from his bhang and said, "Kubera, I do not give relationship advice. Have you ever seen me settle any family matters? That's not my way. You want me to fight Ravana for you, but I can't do that either, because Ravana is totally devoted to me. He's never disturbed me. He completely loves me, supports me, and so do you. You two are brothers, I cannot help you fight amongst yourselves and destroy a tribe. As it is, the Devas and the new emerging species, the *Homo sapiens*, are becoming ever stronger and they're making alliances with each other. So there is no way I'm going to help you fight and destroy your own kind."

"What do I do, Bholenath?" Kubera asked.

Shiva replied, "You want my army? You can have it. My *ganas* will fight for you. But if Ravana comes and asks for the same, I'll have to split the army in half. I'll have to give you half and I'll have to give him the other half. And my *ganas* won't be happy about that, but I can live with that."

Kubera fell at Lord Shiva's feet.

"Hey Gangadhara, Bholenath, O Rudranath!" Kubera said. "You don't need anything, but I do. So please give me a solution. At least I should be able to live properly, maybe not too opulently, but at least somewhat nicely."

"There is only one man who can help you, Kubera," Shiva said. "He is the only sage who will give you unbiased advice because he has received blessings from both me and Vishnu. He has invoked Vishnu as much as he has propitiated me. He is so phenomenal that I had to grant him the boon of immortality. His name is Markandeya."

Kubera then went to sage Markandeya and asked him for advice, if not intervention.

"Ordinarily I would've offered you a meal and shown you the door," Markandeya said, "because this is not something I get myself into. I am an ascetic and you are a king. The things you are involved in don't appeal to me." Markandeya ruminated and then continued, "I can't turn down Shiva's word and I can't do anything for you either. To be honest, had you asked for liberation, I could have and would have helped you. But you are asking for wealth. You are asking me to settle some family disputes. It's not my domain. Therefore, I can't help you."

When Kubera wouldn't relent, Markandeya did what he did best, forwarded Kubera to one of his disciples, the illustrious Medha Rishi, the same one who had guided Suratha and Samadhi.

"He will help you," Markandeya said. "Medha has invoked Divine Mother, the Goddess of opulence, Devi Ma herself. She is also known as Mahalakshmi and Goddess Sri."

When Medha heard of Kubera's plight and saw his despair, he chastised him lovingly. "You are so ignorant!" he said. "You are asking *me* for a solution? Oh, silly boy, do you know that one of your main ancestors was a Yaksha. His name was Pinga. And he had invoked and propitiated Divine Mother. He had pleased her to such a degree that she blessed him with all the wealth in the world. She is the reason why the Yakshas were made the treasurers and not the Rakshasas, although they too lived in the same region. So it was not because your race was superintelligent or good with the numbers, it was because you had Divine Mother's blessings."

"How come no one ever told me about that?" Kubera said.

"Maybe because you were influenced by Sage Pulastya and Vishrava Muni and Bharadwaj's daughter—your mother. All of them belonged to the Devas' clans. They would not have told you the glories of the Yakshas."

When Kubera asked Medha muni what he should do, the rishi said, "I'm going to give you the verse because of which she was called Pingala. When She gave all that wealth and the promise of more eternal wealth to your ancestor, Pinga, she was lovingly given the name Pingala. So you go and invoke Mother Goddess with this verse:

आर्द्रां पुष्करिणीं पुष्टिं पिङ्गलां पद्ममालिनीम् ।
चन्द्रां हिरण्मयीं लक्ष्मीं जातवेदो म आवह ॥

ārdrāṃ puṣkariṇīṃ puṣṭiṃ piṅgalāṃ padmamālinīm ।
candrāṃ hiraṇmayīṃ lakṣmīṃ jātavedo ma āvaha ॥

"You will have to invoke the Devas, you'll have to invoke Agni," Medha instructed. "You'll have to call her with this verse. And when she's happy, you'll be blessed again."

And so it happened that Kubera did intense penance of Sri Suktam and invoked its thirteenth verse. But the ever humble and altruistic Kubera refused to be recognized as the seer of the verse even though he was the one to invoke it. Instead, he insisted that the great sage Medha be acknowledged as the original rishi of this verse. And so it is that to this day, Medha rishi is propitiated as the seer of this verse. As for Kubera, he was blessed abundantly upon the invocation of this verse by none other than the Divine mother herself.

In fact, not only did she bless him, but she also took his case to Vishnu and told him that great injustice had been meted out to a noble Yaksha like Kubera. She averred that Vishnu would have to intervene and do something about it.

So Lord Vishnu appointed Kubera as the official treasurer, while he himself would handle the finances. Kubera went on to build another kingdom, which was even more glorious than Ravana's Lanka, the land for which was donated by Lord Shiva.

Ravana soon set his eyes on even that kingdom. But as time progressed, he conquered and captured vast territories throughout the nation and beyond. And then he got so caught up with the Surpanakha episode mentioned in the Ramayana, that he could not focus on anything else. And before he could capture Kubera's new kingdom, Ravana lost everything he had, including his own life.

Such is the glory of Divine Mother. And as time unfolds, perhaps you will also be as surely intrigued, baffled and grateful as I am every single day. What an amazing hymn this is. And each verse carries such tremendous potency and is invoked by different sages; each of them doing things differently, with different ideas, motives, objectives and purposes to make this hymn what it is.

And that is the beauty of Lord Shiva. You know, he always gives you the right advice. He did tell Kubera that it was Vishnu's Maya and he was getting caught up in it. He did not recommend it but Kubera still went and did what he thought he needed to do at the time.

आर्द्रां यः करिणीं यष्टिं सुवर्णां हेममालिनीम् ।
सूर्यां हिरण्मयीं लक्ष्मीं जातवेदो म आवह ॥१४॥

ārdrāṃ yaḥ kariṇīṃ yaṣṭiṃ suvarṇāṃ hemamālinīm ।
sūryāṃ hiraṇmayīṃ lakṣmīṃ jātavedo ma āvaha ॥ 14 ॥

I am the cherished aim of all the gods and am always in union with Hari. Supporting all the worlds, I also fulfill all desires. I am the substratum of prakriti, the Person and the other cosmic principles. Therefore sages call me yashti, the staff.

I take the successful adepts to the conditional heaven or to the absolute heaven, Hari's sublime abode. The primeval unmanifested beautiful sound denotes me. As the eternal Sarasvati, I express everything beautifully; hence the learned brahmins call me Suvarna.

As the earth, I support the holy golden mountain studded with the moon, sun and planets to provide a befitting dwelling for Brahma. Therefore Virinci, Brahma, praised me by addressing me as Hemamalini.

Attachment Torments Veda Vyasa

Verse 14

The Kuru king Shantanu lost his heart to Satyavati, Veda Vyasa's mother. The same Satyavati who, by virtue of Parashara's boon, smelled not like a fish but fragrant as an exotic flower now. She exuded a heady mix of jasmine, lilies and sandalwood. Hence, she was no longer called Matsyagandhi, but Satyavati. Forget her sight, a mere whiff of her evoked desire in the hearts of men. It was, therefore, no surprise that one day while sport hunting in the woods, a waft of this exotic aroma drove Shantanu mad.

As he moved to the source of the fragrance, he saw the young and lissom Satyavati sitting by the banks of Yamuna, dangling one of her hands in the water. Her other hand was placed on her raised knee, while her youthful face with sharp features was resting sideways on the back of her hand. She looked to be in deep thought.

"I don't know who you are," the king dismounted his horse and spoke to Satyavati, "but whoever you may be, I want to marry you."

Satyavati got up, startled. The back of her palm and knuckles had created an impression on one side of her face. But this dusky beauty was peerless. Shantanu felt like he was dreaming.

He introduced himself as the king of the Kuru kingdom, the most expansive empire in India at the time.

Satyavati realized that the king seemed at least double her age, if not more. For a moment, she felt frustrated that it was her karma to be sought by aging men—first Parashara and now this older king. Also, it was no secret that Shantanu's son, Devavrata was a mighty prince, soon to be anointed the king. *You should be bringing me a proposal for your son and not for yourself.* But she kept her thoughts to herself and told the king that only her father could make that decision.

Satyavati's father, the clever boatman, knew that the rich are eccentric. Once they set their heart on something, they lose all wisdom to negotiate. So when Shantanu approached the boatman, he told the king that to marry his poor daughter would be no different from recreational hunting. Today, he liked Satyavati and another day, he would fall for someone else. To this, Shantanu gave his word that he would never marry another woman, and that Satyavati would not only be his only queen but the empress of the Kuru kingdom.

"I don't doubt your word, O King," the boatman said. "But, the whole world knows that you have a son. Soon, he will be king and will get married; then your promise will have no meaning."

The king went away dejected, but the boatman knew that one way or another, Shantanu would come back. After ferrying all kinds of rich people over the years, he knew that they did not have the capacity to let go of anything they fancied.

Shantanu, however, loved his son Devavrata deeply. He went back to Hastinapur, the capital of India, where he was based. Once back, the lovestruck king lost his appetite and all desire to do anything. Devavrata enquired about, discovered the cause and immediately went to the boatman.

"I will never take up the position of king," Devavrata gave the boatman his word.

"But tomorrow you'll have children and they can dethrone my daughter or her offspring," the boatman argued.

"Then I give you my word that I will forever remain celibate and never marry."

For the young Devavrata to take such a hard pledge—to sacrifice his own pleasures, dreams and joys so that his old father could marry the girl he was desperately in love with—he was given the epithet of Bhishma. The word 'Bhishma' means strong, undeterred, determined and even aggressive to some degree, but also very grounded.

The besotted Shantanu tried to dissuade his son, but only half-heartedly. He eventually agreed to marry Satyavati and sired two sons—Chitrangada and Vichitravirya. Soon afterwards, Shantanu was killed in battle and Chitrangada, too, lost his life at the hands of a Gandharva, a man from the same tribe as Yakshas and Rakshasas.

Vichitravirya was now made king, and he married two princesses called Ambika and Ambalika. As luck would have it, Vichitravirya could never have children and eventually died of a virulent disease within a few years of ascending the throne. All of the boatman's clever planning and Satyavati's desires came to nothing, after all. She was left all alone, with no husband, sons or any heir to the throne. She pleaded with Bhishma to either marry someone and procreate, or to be the king at least; but he reminded her of his lifelong vow of neither becoming a king nor marrying.

Left with no choice, Satyavati summoned her son, the remarkable Veda Vyasa, to help her.

At that time, however, Vyasa was doing a Kaulika sadhana using the left-handed path. And there were certain rules he had to follow, including smearing ash from cremation grounds, living a certain way, not tying his hair and all that. So when he was called, it was a big dilemma for him—should he leave his sadhana midway and go to his mother, or should he continue? In the end, he decided to honor the word he'd given to his mother as a child.

So he interrupted his sadhana to make his way to Hastinapur, where he met his mother, Satyavati, who was so called because her word was the truth and she only spoke the truth. She was a bit taken aback, even terrified, to see her son in such a state, as if he was an *aghori*. But she knew that born from the seed of Parashara, Veda Vyasa was a *tapasvin* like no other. A *mahasiddha* who could shift the movement of time, if he so wished.

"Mother, what can I do for you after all these years?" Vyasa spoke in a calm and solemn voice. "Is everything alright?"

"No, everything is not alright. I need your help," Satyavati said.

"Order."

"My son," Satyavati spoke. "I need you to sire two children with the widowed and childless queens Ambika and Ambalika. If Bharatvarsha is to survive, we need a good king to rule this country."

At first Vyasa tried to tell her that due to his ongoing sadhana, it wasn't the best time for this task, but seeing how insistent Satyavati was, he gave in.

Ambika decked herself up when she was called to visit Veda Vyasa as he sat waiting in a chamber. The moment she saw him, however, she was startled to see a man who looked downright ugly, bearded, with matted locks and a fiery look in his eyes. Veda Vyasa's eyes seemed like glowing embers; terrified, Ambika closed her eyes during the process of procreation. She did not open her eyes even once. As far as she was concerned, this was just something she had to do for territorial, political or moral reasons, to comply with orders that were passed in order to produce an heir to the throne. Veda Vyasa stayed quiet.

Afterwards, Ambalika went into Veda Vyasa's chamber and shuddered deeply on seeing his form. Vyasa was really not dressed to face the world at that time. She too could not handle his fierce looking eyes, face and figure.

Later in the evening, Satyavati asked Veda Vyasa, "Will I have two amazing sons through my two daughters-in-law? Will they be absolutely worthy of being kings?"

"Mother, I did tell you that this was not the best idea but since you insisted, I followed your order," Vyasa spoke with a great deal of concern in his voice. "Ambika closed her eyes during the union, so her son would be born blind. Ambalika became pale in terror. She almost passed out. So her son will be a frail soul. He is going to possess a pale body, always anemic and ready to die at any moment. I am not expecting too much from either of them."

Veda Vyasa took leave and in due course, Ambika gave birth to Dhritarashtra who was born blind. And Ambalika gave birth to Pandu who was always sick and frail.

Since the blind Dhritarashtra and the sickly Pandu were unfit heirs to the throne, Satyavati called Vyasa again to sire another son with Ambika. Reluctantly, Veda Vyasa agreed and she gave her word that Ambika would not close her eyes this time around. Vyasa, too, looked like a magnificent sage, because he was no longer doing the left-handed sadhana. So Satyavati had complete faith that the son born this time around would be one of the wisest and most capable men to ever walk the earth.

Ambika, however, was alarmed as soon as she found out that she had to meet with the frightening Vyasa, again. She wasn't going to take another chance, and so she sent one of her handmaids instead. It was a dark room and Vyasa and the handmaiden couldn't see each other. Vyasa did find it strange that the lady he was with now had no inhibitions or reservations of any kind. She had totally surrendered to the will of the sage and did everything in her power to serve and please him. He blessed her and walked out.

"Will the child be fine this time?" Satyavati asked Vyasa as soon as she saw him.

"This extraordinary child is going to be extremely wise and totally fit to rule," the sage said.

She promised Vyasa that she wouldn't bother him again, and let him go. She was crestfallen, however, upon discovering that Ambika had sent one of her handmaids instead. The son born to the maid was the legendary Vidura. He was the sanest person in the whole of the Kuru kingdom, a frugal but thoughtful speaker, who remained an advisor to the Kuru king till the great war of Mahabharata.

Later, Dhritarashtra would marry the princess of Gandhar called Gandhari and Pandu would take two princesses as his wives—Kunti and Madri.

In Srimad Bhagavatam, Veda Vyasa makes a confession to Devarishi Narada, "Devarishi, I have read all the major scriptures, I did whatever sadhana my father asked me to do. One thing that I am quite guilty of and something I can't forgive myself for, however, is the increasing realization in my heart that I am so attached to the Kingdom of Hastinapur because it is ruled by my children. I feel pathetic when I find myself going there again and again."

Veda Vyasa maintained a constant connection with his sons throughout his life. He had gone there even before the great war happened, and even earlier to warn Draupadi to be careful with her long hair. He had also gone to advise Karna.

"I just don't know what to do, Devarishi," Vyasa said. "Even with all my sadhana, why is it that I am still so attached to my family? You know what happened with Shukadeva. It was so ignorant of me to behave like that. I am an ascetic, and yet I see them as my family. I know it's ignorant, I know it does not befit me. It does not suit me and still here I am. O Narada, how have you remained detached? Please impart me your wisdom."

"How can I give you wisdom?" Narada said. "You are wisdom personified. You are an *avatara* of Lord Vishnu, and I pray to you. You'd better go to your father who is the only one who can advise you. And he is waiting for you. He is still holding on to his body because he needs to speak to you."

Vyasa left to meet with his father, Sage Parashara, immediately. In the years bygone, Parashara's ashram had been attacked a few times. Although Parashara had survived all this while, he had a limp now. That he was old, was evident in every aspect of his appearance, speech and actions. Vyasa bowed before him deeply.

"My son, Krishna Dvaipayan, do you know why I am still in this old body?" Parashara spoke to Vyasa. "I had lost my father, Sage Shakti very early on, and I was brought up by my grandfather, the great Vasishtha. I always knew when you were born that even though I was leaving you behind, you would make a connection with me. You would come back to me. I always thought that whenever that happened, I had to be there for you."

Sage Parashara took a breath, and continued, "So, first things first. Attachment is very natural. I am attached to you and that is why I am still here. I have nobody else in the world and nothing else to live for. But attachment does not mean that it's bad. Attachment depends on how you use it, what you do with that energy of attachment you have. Do you use attachment to shape somebody phenomenal? Or do you use that attachment constantly, just to cling to your loved ones? So I chose the former. And the other reason you are still going through these ups and downs of attachment, guilt, resentment, grudges and so on, is because you have not yet completed your sadhana. Krishna Dvaipayan, all these years have merely been the preparation. I am yet to impart the main sadhana and for that you have to do two things."

Sage Parashara continued, "One, I am going to give you the next verse of Sri Suktam which will bring completion to your sadhana. The first part was simply the beginning—just like you prepare a cloth before it's soaked in colored water for dyeing it. You rub it, you crumple it, you immerse it in water, you pull it out, you dry it, you dip it in water again, you soften it and get rid of all the starch or the particles of dust… All so that when you finally soak it in color and leave it there for a while, it retains the amazing color. Your sadhana, thus far, was just the beginning. Two, I have waited all my life to give you Sri Vidya. So now I am going to give you the whole sadhana of Sri Vidya, starting from Mother divine, the 15 Nityas—Kameshwari to Maha Nitya, and the Vidya is closed with Sri Suktam."

Vyasa became deeply content and happy on hearing his father and he said, "That's all I ever wanted, Father, and now I am going to go away and do the sadhana."

"Yes, but that is not the only reason you were born," Parashara said. "You were already a realized being, an awakened soul. I brought you into this world not so you can procreate for Bharatvarsha. That was just one tiny aspect. That incident happened so that you can build and wield extraordinary political influence in the workings of this nation. I need you to get Atharva Veda—compiled by Atharva rishi—documented properly, and accepted as a mainstream Veda. Your main task is to consolidate the learnings of all the vedas."

Sage Parashara was the author of Vishnu Purana. "Just like me, other sages have written profound scriptures," Parashara continued. "I need you to consolidate these and bring them under one umbrella. Otherwise, this nation, this dharma, will fall apart."

Parashara himself was an exceptional sage whose erudition and scholarship was second to none. He is the man who wrote Hora Shastra, which is the way of interpreting that aspect of astrology where you see how planets move throughout the day in the zodiac, as opposed to *gochara*. To a great degree, he is credited with the discovery of interpreting how planets are moving on a particular day. He wrote the Parashara Samhita, Laghu Parashari, Brihad Parashari, Parashara Hora Shastra and many other monumental works.

"Your word is my command, Father," Vyasa said. "I will carry out the tasks you have set me. I just need your grace and blessings. This will be my life's mission this moment onwards."

"You must not stop going to Hastinapur," Parashara advised Vyasa. "You must maintain constant connection, because the royalty must buy into your philosophy. Only then will this knowledge of the Vedas be spread throughout the nation, and from there, throughout the world.

Vyasa's eyes welled up because looking at his father's advanced age, he wanted to stay back and serve him first. He offered this too, but Parashara declined.

"No, no, no, my son, I have already extended my life a long time," Parashara said. "A painful death awaits me, because I have intervened in the workings of Nature."

"What are you saying?" Vyasa exclaimed, shocked and teary. "What is the purpose of doing your sadhana? What is the result of *my* sadhana if your death is going to be painful?"

"I was supposed to die when the ashram was attacked, but I did not," Parashara replied. "I extended my life. Now some creatures of the forest will take me."

And it so happened that Parashara was once passing through the woods with his disciples when a pack of wolves attacked them. He was a limping old sage, who was frail and couldn't run. His disciples took to their heels, some climbing nearby trees. Sage Parashara saw his death, Kāla, in the form of the wolf. He sat down cross-legged, closed his eyes and went into deep dhyana. The wolves devoured him and did not even leave so much as a fragment of a bone behind.

But he was content in his dying moments, for he had already initiated Vyasa into the most important Vidya and the fourteenth verse of Sri Suktam, which Vyasa brought to life with great penance. True to his word, Veda Vyasa went on to complete his mission. Throughout his life, he consolidated the Vedas, documented the 18 Puranas, Brahma Sutras, Srimad Bhagavatam, and even Devi Bhagavatam. Because he was an ardent and first true worshiper in human form of Sri Vidya, he also created an amazing sadhana with Sri Suktam. He continued with his mission in this country, kept visiting Hastinapur and persisted at all his tasks, till he was last seen by anyone. Vyasa is considered one of the *Chiranjeevis*, immortals, and nobody ever found where he went finally, and what happened to him.

A public holiday, however, was declared in his honor. The festival of Guru Purnima is celebrated in his memory. When the Pandavas became kings, they declared that the full moon of the lunar month of Ashada (that usually falls in July) would be known as Guru Purnima or Vyasa Purnima, and it would be a national holiday. They declared that anything earned on that day would not be taxed. This was woven into the political system of India at the time.

A mention of Sage Parashara is found as early as in the Rig Veda as the seer of many verses found there. Such is the beauty of Sri Suktam which became the basis of Veda Vyasa's sadhana.

तां म आवह जातवेदो लक्ष्मीमनपगामिनीम् ।
यस्यां हिरण्यं प्रभूतं गावो दास्योऽश्वान् विन्देयं पूरुषानहम् ॥१५॥

tāṃ ma āvaha jātavedo lakṣmīmanapagāminīm ।
yasyāṃ hiraṇyaṃ prabhūtaṃ gāvo dāsyo'śvān vindeyaṃ pūruṣānaham ॥ 15 ॥

I alone send the creation forth and again destroy it. I absolve the sins of the good. As the mother earth towards all beings, I pardon them. I mete everything out. I am the thinking process and I am contained in everything. Aware of all these significations of my name, the noble-minded sage Kapila exclaimed: "O Lakshmi, cast thy eyes on me."

I alone become the element of water, being its great, essential, quality, viz. liquidity. In ancient times I, as Sarasvati, requested by Vishvamitra, caused Sage Vasishtha to be carried off in the waters of Sarasvati. When thus the waters of the truthful Sarasvati were about to wash Vasishtha away, the sages addressed me: "O (embodiment of) truth, save the truth-loving Vasistha from the enemies". Then I myself as Sarasvati rescued him from the hands of enemies, and was given the name Anapagamini by the sages.

When Hiranyagarbha Invokes Mother Divine

Verse 15

The great sage Vasishtha was an introvert who preferred a simple life set in an unvarying routine. This was not a reflection on his intellect and ambition. On the contrary, with his peerless scholarship and brilliance, he had been accepted as one of the *saptarishis*, the seven sages. The *saptarishis* formed the governing council that took all major decisions on the legislature of Bharatvarsha, India, at the time. This included the academic curriculum, constitution and various laws. The *saptarishis* were also either traditionally brahmins or in the case of Vasishtha, born to Brahma himself who, being a co-founder of the Vedic constitution, wielded extraordinary influence in the government.

Being not one to socialize, much like his father, Vasishtha would go back to his hermitage after attending these important meetings. He enjoyed the quiet life of a householder with his eight children and his doting wife, Arundhati. Vasishtha was a man of habit. Every day, he would get up before dawn, offer prayers, then write and teach the scriptures, and eat and rest in the afternoon. In the evening, he would spend some time with his family, do his *nitya karma*, and retire for the night. Behind this simple routine, however, was his extraordinary *tapas*, penance, and many *siddhis*, powers, he had acquired over a period of time.

Due to his humility and his simple nature, he was loved by everyone. When the wish-fulfilling cow, Kamadhenu, had appeared at the great churning of the ocean, the governing council of seven sages, *saptarishi*, had unanimously decided to gift it to Vasishtha. He too loved her like his own daughter and never troubled Kamadhenu. But this quiet life was rudely shaken when Vishwamitra, too, became a *brahmarshi*.

Born in the clan of warriors and rulers, a kshatriya, the king Kaushika gave up his wealth and with unrelenting penance ascended to become a brahmarshi—a title that had been exclusive to the most accomplished of sages who were born as brahmins. He was given the name Vishvamitra, a friend of the world. And he was, he stood up for many. But as it happens with the best of the best, a desire overtook him. On a visit to Vasishtha's ashram, he saw Kamadhenu, and from that day onwards, all he wanted was to own the magical cow that was capable of producing any amount of material wealth.

This led to serious conflict between Vishvamitra and Vasishtha. Vishvamitra was adept in the art of battle, strategy, and ruthless about victory—he had been a king all his life, after all. Vasishtha, on the other hand, was the one with powers and knowledge, but he was a family man who just wanted to lead a quiet life away from the world.

Their conflict quickly escalated into full blown acrimony with both resenting the other. Vishvamitra believed that even after becoming a *brahmarshi*, he was not accorded the same respect as other sages, just because he wasn't born a brahmin. He felt like an outsider.

"I disagree," Vasishtha said to Vishvamitra. "If you can do *tapas* like me and invoke the powers of the Universe, you can be whatever you want to be, you can have whatever you want."

"Then give me Kamadhenu," Vishvamitra said petulantly. "I'll do penance later."

"I've told you numerous times, I cannot do that. Kamadhenu is not just any cow, but a daughter to me. You will mistreat her and abuse her to fulfill your territorial ambitions."

Vishvamitra tried to fight Vasishtha, but the latter destroyed his entire army. Not one to forget or let go, Vishvamitra gradually established ties with a tribal community who were also cannibals and belonged to the Rakshasa clan. One day, when Vasishtha was away for the periodic retreat of the governing council, Vishvamitra orchestrated a plan to attack Vasishtha's ashram with the tribal army.

"Kill all his sons and eat them," Vishvamitra ordered Kalmashapada, the chief of the tribe. "If anything of his sons is left behind, Vasishtha would bring them back to life."

Vasishtha upon his return was devastated beyond words. Everything he had worked for his entire life, his family, was no more. And for what? For refusing to fulfill Vishvamitra's demand? This was too much even for the very knowledgable and awakened Vasishtha, who broke down. Eventually, unable to take it anymore, the great Vasishtha decided to jump into the river. He declared that he would not come back; as the river merged in the ocean, he would let his body perish in those briny waters.

Vasishtha felt he had nothing left to live for. He could have dropped his body with the mere power of his yogic prowess, but he did not want the cannibals of the tribe to get hold of his physical body that had been perfected with sadhana and contained the potency of his penance.

Besides, it does not matter how awakened or enlightened one may be, attachment clouds judgment. Vasishtha jumped into a river called Vipasha which later became the present-day river Beas. Meanwhile, the informants of the Devas apprised them of what had taken place. Without losing a moment, they informed Brahma of Vasishtha's action.

Hearing the fate of his son, Brahma was even more distraught than Vasishtha had been. When a foolish child does something irrational, the parents feel frustrated and angry; but when their wise offspring does something stupid, it's hard to get over it. The word 'Vasishtha' means excellent, the best. Brahma knew that in the future his son, Vasishtha, would be the head *purohit*, the head priest of the Ikshavaku clan who were the Suryavanshis, where Vishnu would incarnate as Lord Rama.

Brahma rushed to Vishnu, as governance was his forte and all the jurisdictions fell under him anyway. "Save my son," Brahma pleaded and told Vishnu how proud he had always been of Vasishtha; that it must have been a case of extraordinary injustice if Vasishtha resorted to taking this extreme step.

Lord Vishnu smiled and said, "It seems to me that you've forgotten that my own sons, Chiklīta and Kardama, had already predicted soon after the great churning of the ocean, that this would happen. And that it would be my consort, Lakshmi, who would save your son by splitting the river, for which she would be given the title of Anapagaminim."

Brahma asked, "What should I do? Can you tell me where Vasishtha is? Can you tell me how his future would be?"

"I can't say any of those things, O Hiranyagarbha," Vishnu said. "I only speak about the future when I have to give a boon. For when it comes from me, it's not about what will or won't happen. Whatever I say happens. But I can tell you one thing, your son has something to live for. And for that, you have to propitiate my consort Lakshmi—her sonic form, which is nearly invoked. Just the last two verses are left and when she is fully formed through her Suktam, she will become the basis of material existence, all of it."

"O Vishnu, which verse? How do I go about it?"

"Invoke the fifteenth and sixteenth verses to complete the sonic form of the Goddess," Vishnu said. "Fifteen verses represent the fifteen days of the lunar calendar that run the creation, and because you are the creator, you are responsible to ensure its completion. And the sixteenth verse, because it's the *phalashruti*, the reward, and above all, the sixteenth day represents her glorious form, it's the cusp between the new moon night or the full moon night and the first moon night."

"Vasishtha, even though indirectly," Vishnu continued, "will have an important role to play in the invocation of the full Sri Suktam."

Brahma went away a bit pacified and invoked the fifteenth verse. Mother Goddess appeared before Brahma and said, "This had to happen, O Brahma. This shows how powerful Vishnu's maya is. Look at all these sages like Vishvamitra engaging in actions unbefitting of anyone, let alone them, and somehow feeling territorial about things."

"The only way to keep oneself purified of it is through sadhana," she said. "And sadhana is an ongoing process throughout one's life. Just like the moon waxes and wanes, similarly the human mind ebbs and flows, like the tides of the ocean."

She revealed the location of Sage Vasishtha and said to Brahma, "Go and fetch him. He has come out of the river. I had split the river, so it never went into a tributary or led towards the ocean. He is living like an ascetic. He is quiet and has not spoken since that episode."

"Son, I don't know what the future holds," Brahma said to Vasishtha as soon as he found him, "but I can tell you that you have something to live for, because that's the word of Lord Vishnu himself. Therefore, all I am asking you to do is to go back to your ashram."

Vasishtha said, "Father, there is nothing back there, why would I go to the ashram just so I am once again tormented by those memories? If I go back, I will be haunted by recollections of my children who no longer exist in my life."

Brahma, however, managed to persuade Vasishtha to go back to his ashram. As he walked about the ruins of the once-glorious hermitage, he noticed some smoke coming from a thatched roof and faint Vedic chants sounded. Gobsmacked at any sign of life, Vasishtha rushed to the hut and saw a woman inside. It was his daughter-in-law, Adhrishyanti, the wife of his eldest son, Maharishi Shakti.

"You!" Vasishtha exclaimed in joy. "You are alive, my daughter!"

"The only reason I'm alive, O great sage," she said solemnly, "is because I am carrying your grandson in my womb. When this ashram was attacked, I was down at the river, bringing water for the day and that is why I wasn't discovered by the attackers. I have continued to live here ever since."

Vasishtha was suddenly overcome with the great emotion of love, as well as guilt that he had left his daughter-in-law there alone, to live as she had.

"Who was chanting the Vedas?" Vasishtha asked. "I heard chants."

Adhrishyanti pointed at her belly.

"This grandson of yours has been in there much longer than required. He had heard you and his father chant the Vedas every day. Ever since that episode, I have been chanting the Vedas daily. It's him."

"I'm sorry, my child," he cupped her face and said. "I should have come here earlier like a man, and should not have become so weak. This child will be a great soul. This is what Vishnu must have meant when he said that I have something to live for. I am going to bring up this child!"

That child would become the great sage Parashara. He was called Parashara as it means 'someone who has defied death'. Parashara had every reason not to be alive. Those cannibals had not left anyone alive, yet, somehow, Parashara survived in his mother's womb. Adrishyanti was a great Vedic scholar herself and throughout her pregnancy she chanted the Vedas. Parashara truly defied death. Even when Parashara's own ashram was attacked, he still survived. And when he was attacked again and badly wounded, he still lived, albeit with a limp. In the end, Parashara only gave up his body at a ripe age, when attacked by wolves.

Delighted and grateful that not only did Vasishtha live, but that he would soon have a grandson too, Brahma thanked the Goddess and Vishnu profusely and wholeheartedly accepted the existence of Sri as a sovereign entity, the empress. No one else was truly more suited to invoke the fifteenth and sixteenth verses than Brahma because he was 'the creator' and he existed before all the other people who invoked the Sri Suktam existed.

It is worthy of reflection that Veda Vyasa invoked the fourteenth verse inspired by Parashara and Brahma invoked the later verses of Sri Suktam, verses 15 and 16. One would think that there would be some linearity to it, and Brahma would have invoked earlier ones. But the fact that time is not linear and that the Sri Suktam was invoked over thousands of years were the primary reasons why verses were not invoked in the order they were written. Not to mention, that each verse of Sri Suktam (except the eighth verse, which is not a mantra) is a potent, independent mantra in its own right.

यः शुचिः प्रयतो भूत्वा जुहुयादाज्यमन्वहम् ।
सूक्तं पञ्चदशर्चं च श्रीकामः सततं जपेत् ॥१६॥

yaḥ śuciḥ prayato bhūtvā juhuyādājyamanvaham ।
sūktaṃ pañcadaśarcaṃ ca śrīkāmaḥ satataṃ japet ॥ 16 ॥

The wise, having obtained union with me, experience the fulfilment of each specific desire. Although I have here associated each name and its mantra with what they are specially capable of fulfilling, the intelligent should not assume that they are limited in their capacity to that alone. In fact, Sri Suktam is capable of fulfilling all desires, including liberation.

As this hymn of mine contains a string of names of myself, Sri, its absolute deity, its significance is as unlimited as the stars in the sky, or as gems in the ocean, or as the pleasures of this earth, or as the longed-for objects hanging on the celestial wishing tree, or as the noble characteristics of the cow, or as the brilliant energies of a brahmin, or as the countless divine attributes of Janardana, the supreme God.

Your Story

Verse 16

The final verse of Sri Suktam was invoked by Brahma. Thereafter, it was chanted in full by none other than Lord Vishnu to bring life to the sonic form of Mother Goddess. You know how when two people love each other, they give each other all these endearments? Invoking of the Sri Suktam is no different. As with most other Vedic hymns, we are calling out to the Divine Mother with multiple endearments. We are giving her many names. We are trying to express our love for her in whichever way we can think up.

Sadhana is perhaps the highest expression of true love. For, I don't think that love is just about having intense feelings for someone. In true love you make sacrifices, you watch out for each other and sometimes you do things not because you like them but because you know that the person you love, does.

Bringing Sri Suktam to life is also a labor of love. It requires discipline, sacrifice, responsible freedom and a degree of selflessness. Above all, it needs intense feelings. It doesn't matter how small or big, arcane or mundane your sadhana may be; if there isn't devotion in it, expect no results.

Then again, no sadhana is possible without divine grace. Or for that matter, nothing else is, either. So, when you have the opportunity to do sadhana, it is something to cherish and be grateful for. As you progress on the path, your devotion, focus, stamina, your posture—everything improves. If you are disciplined and devoted, I can tell you with absolute conviction that your sadhana will never go waste. It will yield results at some point in time. It always does.

In the preceding chapters, you might have realized from the stories of amazing sages that grace is unlimited, it's constantly flowing and it's up to you to tap into it. When a stream is gushing vigorously, and you take a vessel to collect some of the running water, you have to be careful at what point you enter the flow. The size of the pot and your placement vis-a-vis the flow of the stream will determine how much will spill versus how much will end up in the vessel. Sadhana is the art and discipline of collecting that stream of grace in a vessel so you may use it to elevate your consciousness and quench the thirst of others in need.

When the results of sadhana manifest in your consciousness, no matter how hard a nut you might have been, the shell cracks open, you become mellow and develop feelings of love and compassion for those around you.

Across the gateway of my heart
I wrote, "No thoroughfare."
But love came passing by
And cried, "I enter everywhere."

—Herbert Shipman

And such is the way of devotion as well, you need a pure heart. The purer the heart, the greater the intensity of the devotion. Otherwise, empty vessels just make a lot of noise.

The other important thing worth remembering when you look at the lives of these amazing sages who invoked the verses, shared in earlier chapters, is that life does not always offer you closure. Often a lot of us think, first I am going to tick off these three items on my to-do list and then I will immerse myself in bhakti and devotion. Or, first I will pay off this debt and then I will do some charity. Or, I am going to take care of these personal issues and then I will embark on my spiritual journey.

But there is no guarantee that life is going to offer you the passage to walk to the end of your journey the way you envisage. Everybody wants their story to end beautifully. A movie can be amazing but if it doesn't end nicely, you say, what was it all about?

Everybody thinks that they are going to tick off these ten things and then when they grow older, are free from familial obligations, and have more savings, they will enjoy themselves; that they will finally sit back and relax. That's when they will put their feet up. But kāla, time, says I will drag you by your feet and take you away.

Never wait for that perfect moment in life, or take life for granted, or assume that such a moment will even arrive in your life. It's ignorant to wait for certain things to finish before you express your gratitude to the Universe, before you do penance and charity.

यज्ञदानतपःकर्म न त्याज्यं कार्यमेव तत् ।
यज्ञो दानं तपश्चैव पावनानि मनीषिणाम् ॥

yajñadānatapaḥkarma na tyājyaṃ kāryameva tat ।
yajño dānaṁ tapaścaiva pāvanāni manīṣiṇām ॥ BG 18.5 ॥

O Kauntaye, one must never relinquish yajna, tapas, sadhana and dāna because they purify you. They are the bedrock of human purification.

So if you think that one day you will grow old (read, be free) and that's when you will do the things that you've always wanted to, it may be a little too optimistic, if not unrealistic altogether. For there is no guarantee that you won't have afflictions, or diseases of the body or the mind. There is no guarantee that you will be able to run or walk or sit, or that your loved ones will still be around. And let me tell you that life will shake you, as is its wont, just as an unexpected earthquake turns everything upside down.

The wise, therefore, seize the present moment and make the best use of it.

Your story is going to be partially influenced by events beyond your control. But that's only partially. There is still a large chunk that is in your control. You owe it to yourself to contribute to your own story. That's the most important story of your life. And the time to do that is now. If you are going to wait, nobody can guarantee what is to come—even a divine sage like Parashara got devoured by the wolves. Vasishtha spent his life in sadhana, and yet his whole family was killed. If you just kept that in mind, I think you would look at life very differently.

You have everything within you that you need to be happy. If you choose to throw that away and not use those assets, that would be a sorry choice, in my humble opinion.

And, it's very important to have the courage to applaud yourself. Most of us hold ourselves in much self-doubt, we demean ourselves, deprecate ourselves and downplay so many of the good things we have worked hard for. We think, *Oh, I don't deserve it.* But it wouldn't happen if you didn't deserve it, good or bad. Love yourself with the same intensity as you would shower on somebody you deeply love. That's all I would say.

There is no next chapter and there are no stories in this one, because now is the time to write your own story in the book of your life. Something beautiful, something magnificent, something meaningful, purposeful, and helpful to humanity. After all, the ultimate purpose of any sadhana is to be able to write (or rewrite) the story of your life.

Go on now, grab that pen and scribble the story you've always wanted to. If not now, then when?

Appendix

The Meaning and Mantras of Sri Suktam

The joy of any journey multiplies once you understand the "why" behind it. Sadhana, too, becomes a sublime practice once you start to realize and appreciate the depth of your endeavor. In the absence of knowing the literal and esoteric meanings of the words you are chanting, much of the sadhana remains a dry exercise, a lifeless pursuit. In this chapter, therefore, I have briefly provided not just the literal translation of all the verses of Sri Suktam but their esoteric meaning too. Further, in Lakshmi Tantra, Divine Mother revealed 53 mantras hidden in the hymn. Such mantras have also been listed here. A sincere seeker can undertake the sadhana of individual mantras too. The simplest way to do the sadhanas of various mantras is to chant the mantra a minimum of 125,000 times. Each mantra of Sri Suktam is capable of elevating your consciousness.

Verse 1

हिरण्यवर्णां हरिणीं सुवर्णरजतस्रजाम् ।
चन्द्रां हिरण्मयीं लक्ष्मीं जातवेदो म आवह ॥१॥

hiraṇyavarṇāṃ hariṇīṃ suvarṇarajatasrajām ।
candrāṃ hiraṇmayīṃ lakṣmīṃ jātavedo ma āvaha ॥ 1 ॥

Invoke for me, O Agni, the Goddess Lakshmi who is radiant like gold, beautiful yellow in hue, adorned with garlands of silver and gold, magnanimous like the moon and an embodiment of wealth and prosperity.

Jātaveda is another name for Agni, fire, and it repeats in the Sri Suktam a total of five times which, by the way, is not a coincidence. The realization of the supreme energy requires that we put our five performatory senses or organs of action (*karmendriyas*) and our five cognitive senses or sense organs (*gyanendriyas*) to the fire of superconsciousness, to rise above these organs. We are forever burned by the five respective fires of actions and senses.

There are seven hidden mantras in this verse, as follows:

1.	ॐ हिरण्यवर्णायै स्वाहा ॥	oṃ hiraṇyavarṇāyai svāhā ॥
2.	ॐ हरिण्यै स्वाहा ॥	oṃ hariṇyai svāhā ॥
3.	ॐ सुवर्णस्रजे स्वाहा ॥	oṃ suvarṇasraje svāhā ॥
4.	ॐ रजतस्रजे स्वाहा ॥	oṃ rajatasraje svāhā ॥
5.	ॐ चन्द्रायै स्वाहा ॥	oṃ candrāyai svāhā ॥
6.	ॐ हिरण्मय्यै स्वाहा ॥	oṃ hiraṇmayyai svāhā ॥
7.	ॐ लक्ष्म्यै स्वाहा ॥	oṃ lakṣmyai svāhā ॥

Verse 2

तां म आवह जातवेदो लक्ष्मीमनपगामिनीम् ।
यस्यां हिरण्यं विन्देयं गामश्वं पुरुषानहम् ॥२॥

tāṃ ma āvaha jātavedo lakṣmīmanapagāminīm ।
yasyāṃ hiraṇyaṃ vindeyaṃ gāmaśvaṃ puruṣānaham ॥ 2 ॥

O Agni! Invoke for me the Goddess who will stay by my side and bless me so I may acquire the material wealth of gold, cows, horses and attendants.

While the Goddess was given the name of Anapagaminim for dividing a river into two rivulets and saving the sage Vasishtha, another meaning of the Sanskrit word *anapagāminīm* means "liquidity". You may have all the wealth in the world but if it's not available for use when you need it, it's not really of much use. Liquidity implies the use of an asset in the immediate term for discharging your fiduciary commitments. Building wealth is one thing but having liquidity is quite another.

Her grace is needed both in terms of liquidity so that you have some income coming in, as well as wealth so you have assets you may use in the future. All other things being equal (such as your skills, relentless effort, etc.), invoking the hidden mantra of this verse helps the seeker align the universal energy so they may build their sources of income. It can also help one dispose of an asset they have been trying to sell for a long time.

The path of sadhana (required to invoke the energy of mantras), however, is difficult and even boring at times. But somewhere, the same holds true for building wealth too. Hardwork is, well, hard, but if you keep walking, you keep progressing.

There is one hidden mantra in this verse, as follows:

1. ॐ अनपगामिन्यै स्वाहा ॥ oṃ anapagāminyai svāhā ॥

Verse 3

अश्वपूर्वां रथमध्यां हस्तिनादप्रबोधिनीम् ।
श्रियं देवीमुपह्वये श्रीर्मा देवी जुषताम् ॥३॥

aśvapūrvāṃ rathamadhyāṃ hastinādaprabodhinīm ।
śriyaṃ devīmupahvaye śrīrmā devī juṣatām ॥ *3* ॥

I invoke Sri, the resplendent Mother Divine who is the Goddess of prosperity, most gloriously accompanied by her retinue of horses in the front, chariots in the middle and whose arrival is announced by the trumpeting of elephants. May she come and bless me.

The esoteric meaning of this verse is reiterated below from the third chapter:

When you embark on the journey of realizing yourself through yogic practices and meditation, in the beginning—if you see how horses run—it is a 'tap-tap-tap-tap' sound you hear within yourself. Once you settle into that rhythm, then emotions, thoughts, desires, temptations, unfulfilled cravings, and so on, will start to rattle your experience. So the middle phase in any sadhana is the most difficult phase. In the beginning you have the energy to say yes, I am going for it. In the middle, you start to question things, so it goes 'gad-gad-gad-gad'—a dull sound. Think of a chariot or a bullock cart moving on an unpaved road, pathway, or a village road. That's the middle sound.

And the third is the 'hhhmmmmm' sound, when the ringing of *anāhat nāda,* the unstruck flowing sound, starts. When you hear this in your heart, it is the most magical experience. It is like conches are blowing, elephants are trumpeting. When you are immersed in sadhana, you will hear distant sounds resonating right within you.

In the churning of the ocean, Uchchaishravas, the horse, came before Airavata, the elephant. Meanwhile, the churning itself was the chariot, the middle stage, the lifelong pursuit of carrying oneself across.

There are six potent mantras found in this verse that are as follows:

1. ॐ अश्वपूर्वायै स्वाहा ॥ oṃ aśvapūrvāyai svāhā ॥
2. ॐ रथमध्यायै स्वाहा ॥ oṃ rathamadhyāyai svāhā ॥
3. ॐ हस्तिनादप्रबोधिन्यै स्वाहा ॥ oṃ hastinādaprabodhinyai svāhā ॥
4. ॐ श्रियै स्वाहा ॥ oṃ śriyai svāhā ॥
5. ॐ मायै स्वाहा ॥ oṃ māyai svāhā ॥
6. ॐ देव्यै स्वाहा ॥ oṃ devyai svāhā ॥

Verse 4

कां सोस्मितां हिरण्यप्राकारामार्द्रां ज्वलन्तीं तृप्तां तर्पयन्तीम् ।
पद्मे स्थितां पद्मवर्णां तामिहोपह्वये श्रियम् ॥४॥

kāṃ sosmitāṃ hiraṇyaprākārāmārdrāṃ jvalantīṃ tṛptāṃ tarpayantīm ।
padme sthitāṃ padmavarṇāṃ tāmihopahvaye śriyam ॥ 4 ॥

I invoke Sri of the lustre of burnished gold, beautiful like the lotus she's seated on, the ever smiling, benevolent, Mother Divine who is the Goddess of prosperity, an embodiment of Absolute Bliss, who is blazing with splendor.

To understand the esoteric meaning of this verse, allow me to elucidate some terms. *Kāṃsosmitāṃ* has two meanings. *Kāṃ*, who has and *sosmitāṃ*, a beautiful smile. *Ārdrā* basically means soft and moist. *Jvalantīṃ*, means something that burns or consumes. *Tṛptāṃ* means something that is satisfied. *Tarpayantīm* is something that satisfies. She is one who is enclosed in a golden enclosure.

We call it wealth when She is enclosed, when you have control over the Goddess somehow. But Her pursuit will consume you, *jvalantīṃ*. Her acquisition is going to somehow offer you temporary fulfillment just like how you get after having a meal, you say, I am *tripta*, satisfied. But you don't say I am content, because contentment is a more sustainable state, which lasts longer. *Tarpayantīm*, through Her you also fulfill all your other desires as well as the desires of others. *Padme sthitāṃ padmavarṇāṃ tāmihopahvaye śriyam*—the one who is situated in a lotus and is of lotus hue, She says that I am, of that. In other words, wealth is made from wealth. You can build material wealth from the wealth of your knowledge, or you can multiply your wealth by putting it in places where it grows (*ārdrā*, in sectors conducive to growth).

There are nine mantras revealed by Divine Mother in this verse, as follows:

1.	ॐ कायै स्वाहा ॥	oṃ kāyai svāhā ॥
2.	ॐ सोस्मितायै स्वाहा ॥	oṃ sosmitāyai svāhā ॥
3.	ॐ हिरण्यप्राकारायै स्वाहा ॥	oṃ hiraṇyaprākārāyai svāhā ॥
4.	ॐ आर्द्रायै स्वाहा ॥	oṃ ārdrāyai svāhā ॥
5.	ॐ ज्वलन्त्यै स्वाहा ॥	oṃ jvalantyai svāhā ॥
6.	ॐ तृप्तायै स्वाहा ॥	oṃ tṛptāyai svāhā ॥
7.	ॐ तर्पयन्त्यै स्वाहा ॥	oṃ tarpayantyai svāhā ॥
8.	ॐ पद्मे स्थितायै स्वाहा ॥	oṃ padme sthitāyai svāhā ॥
9.	ॐ पद्मवर्णायै स्वाहा ॥	oṃ padmavarṇāyai svāhā ॥

Verse 5

चन्द्रां प्रभासां यशसा ज्वलन्तीं श्रियं लोके देवजुष्टामुदाराम् ।
तां पद्मिनीमीं शरणमहं प्रपद्येऽलक्ष्मीर्मे नश्यतां त्वां वृणे ॥५॥

candrāṃ prabhāsāṃ yaśasā jvalantīṃ śriyaṃ loke devajuṣṭāmudārām ।
tāṃ padminīmīṃ śaraṇamahaṃ prapadye'lakṣmīrme naśyatāṃ tvāṃ vṛṇe ॥ 5 ॥

I seek refuge at the lotus feet of the Goddess who is as beautiful and bright as the moon, who blazes with illustriousness, who is adored by the gods and exceedingly munificent. May my misfortunes end, I invoke thee.

In Lakshmi Tantra, the Goddess states that She is the radiance of the moon. She is *candrāṃ prabhāsāṃ*, the light of the moon which is simply a reflection of the sun. Similarly, with sadhana, the yogin starts to carry Her reflection in his/her heart. Such compassionate and loving reflection is enough to heal many lives including one's own. Calling Herself *prabhāsāṃ yaśasā jvalantīṃ*, She says just how you need butter in a lamp to keep it going, you need Her to keep your life going. Invoking this verse or the hidden mantras of this verse bestows upon the sadhak constant blessings of the Goddess in the form of material prosperity.

There are a total of eight mantras hidden in this verse. They are as follows:

1. ॐ चन्द्रायै स्वाहा ॥ — oṃ candrāyai svāhā ॥
2. ॐ प्रभासायै स्वाहा ॥ — oṃ prabhāsāyai svāhā ॥
3. ॐ यशसायै स्वाहा ॥ — oṃ yaśasāyai svāhā ॥
4. ॐ ज्वलन्त्यै स्वाहा ॥ — oṃ jvalantyai svāhā ॥
5. ॐ देवजुष्टायै स्वाहा ॥ — oṃ devajuṣṭāyai svāhā ॥
6. ॐ उदारायै स्वाहा ॥ — oṃ udārāyai svāhā ॥
7. ॐ तायै स्वाहा ॥ — oṃ tāyai svāhā ॥
8. ॐ पद्मनेम्यै स्वाहा ॥ — oṃ padmanemyai svāhā ॥

Verse 6

आदित्यवर्णे तपसोऽधिजातो वनस्पतिस्तव वृक्षोऽथ बिल्वः ।
तस्य फलानि तपसानुदन्तु मायान्तरायाश्च बाह्या अलक्ष्मीः ॥६॥

ādityavarṇe tapaso'dhijāto vanaspatistava vṛkṣo'tha bilvaḥ ।
tasya phalāni tapasānudantu māyāntarāyāśca bāhyā alakṣmīḥ ॥ 6 ॥

O Mother Divine, resplendent as the sun! As a result of thy glories and penance have the sacred plants like bilva come into existence. May the fruits of (such penance) destroy all inauspiciousness arising out of my impure thoughts and ignorant actions.

Reflecting upon the esoteric meaning of this verse, you realize that *bilva* here represents the purest knowledge that has sprouted after piercing the ground of afflictions and impurities. In fact, in *Yoga Vasishtha*, Sage Vashistha explains to Rama, "O Rama, the Bilva is actually a very special fruit. It is beyond destruction, and it is even bigger than the universe. You must have heard of Hiranya Garbha; the *bilva* fruit also has the same existence." And then Lord Rama said, "I understand what you mean by the (significance of the) *bilva* fruit. It represents the purest knowledge, because it is (symbolic of a state which is) beyond the dualities. I know what you mean. The fruit that Mother was going to offer to rise above dualities was the fruit of pure wisdom. O Sage Vasishtha, when you talk about the Bilva fruit are you referring to what is *sat*—the purest, finest wisdom, pure *jñāna*, that is needed to rise above any form of dualities? I understand now, that is why Lord Shiva loves this fruit because it represents the ultimate form of liberation which comes due to *tapas* and sadhana."

Invoking this verse or the hidden mantra in it is particularly useful to purify one's consciousness. The one mantra found in this verse is as follows:

1. ॐ आदित्यवर्णायै स्वाहा ॥ oṃ ādityavarṇāyai svāhā ॥

Verse 7

उपैतु मां देवसखः कीर्तिश्च मणिना सह ।
प्रादुर्भूतोऽस्मि राष्ट्रेऽस्मिन् कीर्तिमृद्धिं ददातु मे ॥७॥

upaitu māṃ devasakhaḥ kīrtiśca maṇinā saha ।
prādurbhūto'smi rāṣṭre'smin kīrtimṛddhiṃ dadātu me ॥ 7 ॥

With thy grace, O Mother! I'm living in a blessed country. May Kubera (the guardian lord of wealth) and kirti (fame) come to me. May the Gods bestow upon me fame and prosperity.

Often, we don't know how attached we are to something until we are separated from it. Similarly, even though a good seeker deeply desires to be self-realized, and they believe that they don't really have worldly desires, the fact is it's hard to ascertain the truth in the absence of abundance. It is easy to say and feel that we are not attached to wealth when we have very little to begin with. On the path of Sri Suktam sadhana, twice the aspirant is blessed with material abundance. The first time is a test. A lot of seekers get comfortable in the material world, losing sight of their goal. Their spiritual progress stops right there. But those who keep walking the path of awakening may choose to walk away from the material pursuits, but the Goddess ensures that they are blessed with opulence and abundance once again.

Invoking this verse or the hidden mantras in it evokes feelings of intense gratitude in the mind of the seeker. Such disposition then acts as a potent bait to attract wealth and material fame. For, a grateful heart is naturally more positive and makes you more effective at everything you undertake. The two mantras found in this verse are as follows:

1.	ॐ कीर्त्यै स्वाहा ॥	oṃ kīrtyai svāhā ॥
2.	ॐ ऋद्धयै स्वाहा ॥	oṃ ṛddhayai svāhā ॥

Verse 8

क्षुत्पिपासामलां ज्येष्ठामलक्ष्मीं नाशयाम्यहम् ।
अभूतिमसमृद्धिं च सर्वां निर्णुद मे गृहात् ॥८॥

kṣutpipāsāmalāṃ jyeṣṭhāmalakṣmīṃ nāśayāmyaham । abhūtimasamṛddhiṃ ca sarvāṃ nirṇuda me gṛhāt ॥ 8 ॥

With thy grace and my efforts, I shall ward off inauspiciousness and distressing poverty in the form of hunger, thirst, and the like. O Lakshmi! Dispel from my home every misfortune and insufficiency.

There are no individual mantras for chanting in this verse for the simple reason that positive affirmations focusing on growth and evolution are more aligned to the workings of the Universe than affirmations born out of insecurity and fear. In other words, "O Universe, help me lead a life of love and compassion" is more powerful a prayer than, say, "O Universe, do not let me be full of hate and apathy".

And as such, this verse of Sri Suktam that focuses on warding off inauspiciousness has no mantras to chant. For the Universe does not understand what you "don't" want. It only reads the energy you are trying to put into anything. Or simply put, it only understands the one thing you desperately want.

Verse 9

गन्धद्वारां दुराधर्षां नित्यपुष्टां करीषिणीम् ।
ईश्वरीं सर्वभूतानां तामिहोपह्वये श्रियम् ॥९॥

gandhadvārāṃ durādharṣāṃ nityapuṣṭāṃ karīṣiṇīm ।
īśvarīṃ sarvabhūtānāṃ tāmihopahvaye śriyam ॥ 9 ॥

I invoke Sri, the Mother Divine, who is the supreme controller of all beings, who can be perceived through heady fragrance, who is beyond defeat and threat, who is ever virtuous and abundant.

Basically, the phrase '*gandhadvārām durādharshām*' means: "O divine Mother! You carry yourself through fragrance and you are *durādharshām*, invincible, irresistible, you cannot be attacked." *Nityapushtām* simply means that every day, you are taking care of your creation. *Pushti karna* means confirmation, but it also means to strengthen something, to nourish something.

Explaining what *karīshinīm* is, the Mother says, "There are only three places where I go; because of that I have been given the term '*karīshinīm*' by scholars. *Yagya,* good karma; *daan,* charity; and *adhyayan*, study—these are my three prime and chief good uses, *sātvik* uses." The phrase '*īshwarīm sarvabhūtānām*' means: "Mother, You are the presiding, governing force of everything there is." *Tamiho upahvaye shriyam* means: "I am calling upon You, please be beside me!"

More about the term *gandhadwārām*—you know how it is with fragrance, you can feel it… you can perceive it? It can make you feel a certain way, it can evoke certain memories in you, certain emotions, but you can't hold onto it… you can't hold on to fragrance. You may put it in a bottle of perfume through various methods; you might capture it just the way you would capture energy through mantras, and when you use it, it brings the same fragrance. So the Divine Mother says, "Look Indra, Purandara, I am elusive like fragrance, I make everything beautiful but I am not something or somebody you can hold on to!"

The five hidden mantras found in this verse are as follows:

1. ॐ गन्धद्वारायै स्वाहा ॥ om̐ gandhadvārāyai svāhā ॥
2. ॐ दुराधर्षायै स्वाहा ॥ oṃ durādharṣāyai svāhā ॥
3. ॐ नित्यपुष्टायै स्वाहा ॥ oṃ nityapuṣṭāyai svāhā ॥
4. ॐ करीषिण्यै स्वाहा ॥ oṃ karīṣiṇyai svāhā ॥
5. ॐ ईश्वर्यै स्वाहा ॥ oṃ īśvaryai svāhā ॥

Verse 10

मनसः काममाकूतिं वाचः सत्यमशीमहि ।
पशूनां रूपमन्नस्य मयि श्रीः श्रयतां यश ॥ १० ॥

manasaḥ kāmamākūtiṃ vācaḥ satyamaśīmahi ।
paśūnāṃ rūpamannasya mayi śrīḥ śrayatāṃ yaśaḥ ॥ 10 ॥

O Mother Divine, Goddess of prosperity! May we enjoy the fulfilment of our noble desires, may we be blessed with veracity of speech, wealth and abundant foodgrains. May prosperity and fame reside in Thy devotee.

Much like the seventh verse earlier, this verse also focuses on ensuring that the seeker is blessed with prosperity and abundance. Just as a mother would never want her children to go hungry or be deprived of the goodness of life in any way, true worship of Mother Goddess naturally brings wealth and prosperity in one's life. A small child, however, finds her mother's lap the safest place on earth. And that's just about the only thing where this verse varies from the seventh. That is, in that verse the seeker desired name, fame, and wealth. In this one, while the seeker is asking for abundance, he understands that the ultimate treasure is the goddess herself.

Basically, *manasaḥ kāmam ākūtiṃ* means "my heart truly yearns for you, O Divine Mother". And manasaḥ kāmam also indicates "all that my heart desires". *Vācaḥ satyamaśīmahi,* signifies that all my words should be truthful and they should reach you. Everything I say is designed to reach you. My speech, my very being, truly just wants you.

All animate existence, including human beings, is known as *paśū*. So *paśūnām rupam* implies all beauty, all existence including all those things which used to be considered as opulence in the heydays (ancient times), which would be cattle and horses and so. All this wealth is only in your refuge.

Invoking this verse or the mantras of this verse blesses the seeker with superior consciousness and abundance in their life. The five mantras revealed by Divine Mother in this verse are as follows:

1.	ॐ मनसः कामाय स्वाहा ॥	oṃ manasaḥ kāmāya svāhā ॥
2.	ॐ वाच आकूत्यै स्वाहा ॥	oṃ vāca ākūtyai svāhā ॥
3.	ॐ पशूनां रूपाय स्वाहा ॥	oṃ paśūnāṃ rūpāya svāhā ॥
4.	ॐ सत्याय स्वाहा ॥	oṃ satyāya svāhā ॥
5.	ॐ अन्नस्य यशसे स्वाहा ॥	oṃ annasya yaśase svāhā ॥

Verse 11

कर्दमेन प्रजाभूता मयि सम्भव कर्दम।
श्रियं वासय मे कुले मातरं पद्ममालिनीम्॥११॥

kardamena prajābhūtā mayi sambhava kardama ।
śriyaṃ vāsaya me kule mātaraṃ padmamālinīm ॥ 11 ॥

O Kardama! Make her abide with me. Make the Goddess of Prosperity who is the mother of the Universe and wears garlands of lotuses, dwell in our family.

Kardamena implies two things here. One is self evident, that it is the name of the sage Kardama and we are calling upon the Goddess from whom Kardama emerged. The meaning and term which is more relevant here is, *kardamena prajabhuta*, meaning moist earth and all that has come out of that earth, which is pretty much everything, one way or the other. And *shriyam*, also means to be with us, to be close and to make it possible, and to have that union. *Shriyamvāsaya me kule, mataram padmamalinim*—may the grace of Divine Mother always be there in my clan and in the world.

This verse and its mantras are invoked purely for the blessings of the Goddess. The desire here is not to have material abundance or the rest of it, but simply to have the grace of the Divine Mother coursing through our lives at all times.

There are two mantras in this verse:

1. ॐ मात्रे स्वाहा॥ oṃ mātre svāhā ॥
2. ॐ पद्ममालिन्यै स्वाहा॥ oṃ padmamālinyai svāhā ॥

Verse 12

आपः सृजन्तु स्निग्धानि चिक्लीत वस मे गृहे।
नि च देवीं मातरं श्रियं वासय मे कुले॥१२॥

āpaḥ sṛjantu snigdhāni ciklīta vasa me gṛhe ।
ni ca devīṃ mātaraṃ śriyaṃ vāsaya me kule ॥ 12 ॥

Let the waters produce oily products (like butter) in my house. O Chiklīta, dwell in my house and make the Goddess of Prosperity, the Divine Mother, also dwell in my family.

You know, they say that wherever the calf goes, the mother goes; the cow follows its calf (and vice-versa). In the previous verse, we called upon the sage Kardama. In this verse, however, we are referring to sage Chiklīta, saying "Oh, Mother Divine! Please be a part of our family. I am a householder and to live in this world, to be sane, to have a constant sense of belonging and a loving environment, I need to have a family. And because I'm a householder, I cannot abandon my family and go in pursuit of viewing the divine. So You have to descend into my world. '*Ni cha devī mātaram sriyam vāsaya me kule*' signifies: "Please Devi, come here and live amongst us and be with us."

Since Chiklīta and Kardama emerged at the time of the churning of the ocean, they are also considered *manas-putras* of Vishnu, offspring created from the mind of Vishnu. The esoteric meaning of Chiklīta in this verse is: all that is created from mind. Chiklīta also refers to the moist nature of water (while Kardama means soft ground). Invoking verses 11 and 12 creates conducive conditions in one's life for all material and spiritual pursuits.

This verse has no mantras revealed by the Divine Mother.

Verse 13

आर्द्रां पुष्करिणीं पुष्टिं पिङ्गलां पद्ममालिनीम् ।
चन्द्रां हिरण्मयीं लक्ष्मीं जातवेदो म आवह ॥ १३ ॥

ārdrāṃ puṣkariṇīṃ puṣṭiṃ piṅgalāṃ padmamālinīm ।
candrāṃ hiraṇmayīṃ lakṣmīṃ jātavedo ma āvaha ॥ 13 ॥

O Jātaveda! Bring to me the extremely benign Lakshmi who is reddish in complexion, who dwells in lakes and who possesses the Moon's brilliance and gold in abundance.

Ārdram means moist, tender, and benign. If you have ever observed the process of boring the earth, when we want to get water out of it, a lot of things come out during this procedure. Initially, you'll get some stones and some pebbles which occur in the top layer of the earth. Then, as you go deeper, you find more stones, you get a lot of mud, a lot of earth; and as you dig even deeper, you actually find a lot of moist earth turning up. You keep going and you'll get sand. As you keep digging, you'll strike a bit of water, but it's not clean. Upon still further excavation you get more and more sand; finally, when you keep going, you eventually hit the purest water source.

Now, when the great churning of the ocean happened, the substances that came out were pretty much at par with the substances we find when we actually bore any part of the earth. This just goes to show how real the massive operation must have been. It's a little hard to say for sure, but what was being churned might have been the vast ocean, or maybe a large water body.

In Lakshmi Tantra, the Mother Divine states that She is called *pushkarinīm*, from the wheel of time which is known as *pushkar*. She says, "The wheel of time is like a flower, and I am the one who governs it. Therefore, the gods gave me the name *pushkarinīm*. And I am known as *pushtim* since I nourish everybody." She is also called *pingalām* and it's a beautiful word—it means a shade of burnished burnt red, not exactly yellow.

Once again, this verse is invoked by Medhas Rishi, who also invoked the ninth verse. He requests, "Please bring me that Mother Goddess who has a very benign and soft presence". He's not asking to be given wealth, or anything else material. Instead he pleads: just be here with me and that is enough.

The mantras contained in this verse are as follows:

1. ॐ पुष्करिण्यै स्वाहा ॥ om̤ puṣkariṇyai svāhā ॥
2. ॐ पुष्टये स्वाहा ॥ oṃ puṣṭaye svāhā ॥
3. ॐ पिङ्गलायै स्वाहा ॥ oṃ piṅgalāyai svāhā ॥

Verse 14

आर्द्रां यः करिणीं यष्टिं सुवर्णां हेममालिनीम् ।
सूर्यां हिरण्मयीं लक्ष्मीं जातवेदो म आवह ॥ १४ ॥

ārdrāṃ yaḥ kariṇīṃ yaṣṭiṃ suvarṇāṃ hemamālinīm ।
sūryāṃ hiraṇmayīṃ lakṣmīṃ jātavedo ma āvaha ॥ 14 ॥

O Jātaveda! Bring to me the extremely benign Lakshmi of a golden complexion who dwells in lakes, who is the bestower of plenty, who wears a garland of gold, who is resplendent like the sun and abounds in wealth.

The Divine Mother says, "I am the cherished aim of all the gods there are. I am eternally united with Sri Hari. I support all worlds, hence I have been referred to as '*ārdrāṃ yaḥ kariṇīṃ yaṣṭiṃ*'. She declares, "I am the substratum of all there is, the underlying substance—even the underlying layers of Purusha and Prakriti. That's why sages called me *yashtim* or *yashtaye*, which means to support—a staff or stick."

Kariṇīṃ means: 'she makes it possible', but interestingly, *kariṇīṃ* in Rigveda also refers to a female elephant. While She is surrounded by two bull elephants who guard her and stand in service, She is shown to live in a cow elephant, making creation and procreation possible.

The line '*sūryāṃ hiraṇmayīṃ lakṣmīṃ jātavedo ma āvaha*' can be interpreted as: "O Mother Goddess, You have the radiance of the sun itself." Why, in Lalita Sahasranama, her effulgence is compared to that of a thousand radiant suns (*udayatbhānu sahasrābhā*).

Krishna too says in the Bhagavad Gita:

न तु मां शक्यसे द्रष्टुमनेनैव स्वचक्षुषा ।
दिव्यं ददामि ते चक्षु: पश्य मे योगमैश्वरम् ॥११:८॥

na tu māṃ śakyase draṣṭumanenaiva svacakṣuṣā
divyaṃ dadāmi te cakṣuḥ paśya me yogamaiśwaram ॥ BG 11:8 ॥

O Arjuna, you can't see me with these eyes, so don't kill yourself trying to do it. You may be good at shooting and at archery and all that, but this is totally different. Hence I am going to give you a different set of eyes.

There are four mantras contained in this verse as follows, completing the revelation of 53 mantras of the divine hymn of Sri Suktam:

1.	ॐ यष्टये स्वाहा ॥	oṃ yaṣṭaye svāhā ॥
2.	ॐ सुवर्णायै स्वाहा ॥	oṃ suvarṇāyai svāhā ॥
3.	ॐ हेममालिन्यै स्वाहा ॥	oṃ hemamālinyai svāhā ॥
4.	ॐ सूर्यायै स्वाहा ॥	oṃ sūryāyai svāhā ॥

Verse 15

तां म आवह जातवेदो लक्ष्मीमनपगामिनीम् ।
यस्यां हिरण्यं प्रभूतं गावो दास्योऽश्वान् विन्देयं पूरुषानहम् ॥ १५॥

tāṃ ma āvaha jātavedo lakṣmīmanapagāminīm ।
yasyāṃ hiraṇyaṃ prabhūtaṃ gāvo dāsyo'śvān vindeyaṃ pūruṣānaham ॥ 15 ॥

O Jātaveda! Bring to me that Lakshmi who will not forsake me and by whose grace I may obtain in plenty gold, cows, maids, horses and servants.

Imagine drawing a line on a rock. Now imagine doing that every day, several times a day, over and over again for several years. Eventually, that line will be engraved so deeply in that rock that if you poured water on that rock, it would automatically flow through the crevice created by years of drawing the same line at the same place. One of the basic principles of the science of mantras is repetition. That is, in invoking a mantra with devotion, we rely on something similar: the power of repetition. Hence, it is no surprise that in this verse the seeker is simply reinforcing what they have asked throughout the suktam, that is, Divine Mother's grace and material abundance (*prabhūtaṃ).*

There are no new mantras in this or the next verse of Sri Suktam.

Verse 16

यः शुचिः प्रयतो भूत्वा जुहुयादाज्यमन्वहम् ।
सूक्तं पञ्चदशर्चं च श्रीकामः सततं जपेत् ॥ १६॥

yaḥ śuciḥ prayato bhūtvā juhuyādājyamanvaham ।
sūktaṃ pañcadaśarcaṃ ca śrīkāmaḥ satataṃ japet ॥ 16 ॥

He who is desirous of becoming prosperous should, after making himself pure and controlling his senses, make daily offerings of melted butter in the fire. He should also repeat always the above stanzas of mantras.

This verse is *phala-shruti,* a declaration of reward. From my experience of more than three decades of sadhana, I can tell you that complete mental worship of Sri Suktam is as effective as making physical offerings, if not even more effective. In the next section, I have given four ways to invoke Sri Suktam so you may receive benefit from this sublime sadhana.

If you would like to know more, I recommend you read the English translation of Lakshmi Tantra by Sanjukta Gupta. It's very well done. In fact, at the beginning of each chapter in this book, I have provided an exposition of each verse of Sri Suktam. They have been directly taken from Sanjukta Gupta's translation of Lakshmi Tantra.

Performing the Sadhana of Sri Suktam

If after reading this book, you now wish to undertake the sadhana of Sri Suktam, you have come to the right place. There are four ways to do the sadhana of Sri Suktam. They vary based on difficulty level and intensity. Consequently, the results too vary in terms of effectiveness and impact. I have listed all the four methods for you, as follows:

1. Nitya Karma (Daily Routine)

Difficulty level: Beginner.
Effectiveness: Noticeable impact over a long term
Prerequisite: None

This method involves chanting the Sri Suktam at least once every day. There are no tedious methods or rituals. Simply recite the Sri Suktam as part of your daily prayers. You can do so in the morning, afternoon, evening, or night. Done with devotion (and understanding of Sri Suktam—which you now possess after reading this book), it helps you build a personal bond with Mother Goddess eventually allowing you to tap into a constant flow of grace. Even if you choose one or more of the three methods below, I still highly recommend making daily chanting a part of your everyday prayer regime.

2. Regular Sadhana of 16 Nights

Difficulty level: Medium
Effectiveness: High over medium to long term
Prerequisite: None

The Sri Suktam sadhana of 16 nights is an awakened and potent sadhana that is usually started on the night of Diwali. But you can also start it on any new moon night of any month and complete it over the next 16 nights. The more you can do, the better for you. Having performed this sadhana numerous times over the last three decades, I have simplified the process for you greatly. You can access the method, process and detailed notes alongwith FAQs for free on my blog os.me/sri-suktam-sadhana/

3. Elaborate Sadhana of 16 Nights

Difficulty level: Expert
Effectiveness: Very high even in the short to medium term
Prerequisite: 1000 chants of Sri Suktam performed over 1000 days (one-a-day).

In my book *The Ancient Science of Mantras*, I have explained in minute detail the whole science of mantras, and most notably, the most precise method of invoking Sri Suktam. This is the method I had used during my sadhana of Sri Suktam. If you wish to delve deeper into Mantras, you can read the book. But, if you just want to access the chapter of performing the Sri Suktam sadhana with the elaborate method, I have put the entire chapter online for free. This is an independent chapter and the notes are complete in themselves. You can download the PDF by going to os.me/elaborate-method-sri-suktam-sadhana-pdf

4. Join me live on Sadhana App

Difficulty level: Lowest possible
Effectiveness: Very high
Prerequisite: None

Every year, thousands of seekers join me live on the Sadhana app to perform this sadhana in the most immersive manner. Like everything else I do, it is 100% free. It is perhaps the highest form of most effective, *manasik pooja*, mental worship, where you offer all the ingredients digitally, live, in real time. While it is a technological marvel, the actual sadhana and yajna is done in a most ancient fashion. Simply download the free Sadhana app to do the Sri Suktam sadhana. Every year, we start it on Diwali. (You can do other amazing sadhanas in the app throughout the year).

As I say always, "*Sadhana se sambhav hai.*" It's possible with sadhana. I hope you go on to reap incredible rewards from the power of sadhana.

Sri Matre Namah.